Girl in a Blue Bonnet

Girl in a Blue Bonnet

The true story of a woman's quest in Africa

Dot Scott

authorHOUSE®

AuthorHouse™
1663 Liberty Drive
Bloomington, IN 47403
www.authorhouse.com
Phone: 1-800-839-8640

First published by AuthorHouse   09/15/2011

ISBN: 978-1-4670-2616-1 (sc)
ISBN: 978-1-4670-2617-8 (ebk)

Library of Congress Control Number: 2011916310

Printed in the United States of America

Any people depicted in stock imagery provided by Thinkstock are models, and such images are being used for illustrative purposes only.
Certain stock imagery © Thinkstock.

Back cover background image: Jens Beste, www.joshushund.com

This book is printed on acid-free paper.

This book is dedicated to my husband Doug, our children Gary, Michael, Alan and Julie, their spouses Zelda, Tish, Karen and John, and our ten grandchildren, Mitchell, Matthew, Paige, Jessica, Roxanne, Tandia, Hayley, Rowan, Luke and Warren, who bring sunshine into our lives.

This is the true life story of Major Mrs. Daisy Scott (nee Quarterman), who served as an Officer in the Salvation Army in South Africa from 1896 for forty-two years, during some of the country's most turbulent times. The names of towns and countries relate to the period in history covered by this book.

Her life story was originally published in serial form in the Salvation Army's magazine, *The War Cry*, in Cape Town, South Africa, in 1975.

Acknowledgments

Grateful thanks to Ray Lecolle-Brown of South Africa for detailed Scott family tree and information, Ray Quartermain of the Netherlands for invaluable information concerning the Quarterman and Quartermain families, and Mike Scott and Julie Termuende for encouragement and technical assistance. Also to Carol Gardarsson, Mary-Ellen Turner, Maureen Silver and Niv Harris for editing, and Captain Diane Cross, of the Salvation Army in Gibsons B.C. for assistance with the book.

CHAPTER 1

THAT EVENTFUL SPRING OF 1878

"Spring!" muttered James Quarterman, shrugging into his heavy overcoat. He peered into the hallstand mirror to adjust his scarf. "Seems more like winter's come back—and it's already the seventeenth of April," he remarked to his eleven-year-old daughter Nellie, ready to hand him his cap.

"It's awful," agreed Nellie, "I'll never be able to find my way to school in this thick mist. Daisy's lucky. She doesn't have to go outside at all. She can keep warm by the fire."

James detected just a note of jealousy in Nellie's remarks.

"Daisy is only eight weeks old, Nellie," he reminded her, as his wife came into the hall from the kitchen, wiping her hands on her apron.

Amelia sighed as she glanced through the hall window. Beyond it loomed an elm tree, shrouded in wisps of cotton wool mist, the daffodils at its trunk trying bravely to paint a bright splash of colour onto the drab scene. England's April weather could be unpredictable. She shivered, drawing her shawl closer around her shoulders.

"Just wait one moment while I fetch Daisy," she said, going to the parlour. She lifted the baby from her crib, tucked a small blanket around her, and held her out to her husband. He kissed the tiny pink cheek, then turning to Nellie he put his strong arm around her shoulders and hugged her.

"Well, I must be off," James said. "Be careful crossing the road, Nellie, the mist is so thick you'll scarcely be able to see in front of you."

"Good-bye my dear," he said, then kissed Amelia. He paused to look down once more at the baby in Amelia's arms. Daisy was the eleventh child to be born to Amelia and James, seven of them having died in infancy or early childhood.

Although his family was doubtful whether this baby would live for long, James was convinced she would. She seemed to have a strong will already. She'll survive, he thought, and make something worthwhile of her life.

"In a year's time she'll be toddling across the room, bringing me my slippers when I come home from work," he remarked.

With a cheery "good-bye" he opened the door and set off for work, the mist enveloping his tall figure as he followed the path that led over the railway line to the Ealing Post Office on the other side of the railway station.

Amelia and James Quarterman with Mary (Polly) standing,
Ellen (Nellie), James Jr and Olive.

James lived a very busy life, thankful for whatever work he could find during Britain's high rate of unemployment in 1878. By day he worked at the Post Office and in the evening tended to the Methodist Church and its grounds, in exchange for the use of the caretaker's cottage.

He always left home early, giving himself plenty of time to cross the railway line before the first train was due at the station. But now, as the dampness of the mist hung around him, making walking unpleasant, he hurried more quickly than usual, past the rows of brick houses to the meadow alongside the railway line.

On that fateful day, however, he could not have known that an additional engine was on its way to the station, bearing the body of a man killed further up the line. Nor did he realize that the signalman had negligently failed to signal its approach.

James was already crossing the railway line when he suddenly heard the loud whistle of a train and the hissing of steam as it emerged giant-like out of the mist. A monster coming straight for him! Wide eyed, he stood transfixed with fear.

The horrified engine driver applied the brakes. Desperately James tried to jump clear of the track, but it was too late. With a violent thud the engine struck him, flinging his body through the air. He sprawled, lifeless, alongside the railway line as the train thundered by.

Once the protesting Nellie had reluctantly departed for school, Amelia took Daisy back into the parlour and sank down onto the sofa beside the fire, grateful for the warmth and cosiness of the caretaker's cottage.

Looking down at the sleeping baby in her arms, she felt a sense of gratitude that this infant seemed fairly healthy, despite her delicate appearance, and she hoped fervently that she would survive. She knew only too well the pain of losing a child. They had lost five babies shortly after they were born, their son John at the age of ten, and their daughter Olive, aged eight, who had died after an illness only four years previously. Olive's death had left Nellie, then seven years old, completely devastated.

So much had happened in their lives since she, a member of the Dumbleton family, had married James Quarterman in the Independent Chapel in Ealing, on October 11th, 1853. Looking back on their wedding day, Amelia smiled as she remembered how the sun had come briefly through the clouds on that autumn day, as if to bless their union. She and her father, John Dumbleton, had arrived by horse and cart, driving slowly past Wisteria Cottage, built in 1824 in his quiet street, and other picturesque cottages framed by an avenue of yew trees on Ealing Green.

Waiting quietly in the chapel were her mother Mary, James' father John Quarterman, his wife Elizabeth, her brother Henry and other family members. Although this was a small wedding, Amelia and James were happy as their eyes met.

They had such high hopes for the future. James had a job repairing shoes, working for a shoemaker in Ealing, and with plans to start his own shoemaking business. This would enable Amelia to give up her position as a servant, and devote her time to making a home for them.

Over the years James built up his shoemaking business, then later owned a grocery store that he ran for several years until larger stores forced him out of business. Amelia, meanwhile, was kept busy with their children. Bringing them up had not been easy during their twenty-four years of marriage, but now they were blessed again, when at the age of forty-eight years, Amelia gave birth to Daisy. Arriving so late in life, this little baby truly was a gift from God, Amelia mused.

Amelia's thoughts were abruptly brought back to the present when she was surprised by a sudden knock at the front door.

Placing Daisy gently in her crib, she hurriedly removed her apron and walked to the front door.

"I wonder who's visiting at this hour," she exclaimed, "it's only ten o'clock in the morning!"

One look at the faces of the two men standing at the door brought a feeling of uneasiness, as Amelia invited them indoors. The Methodist Minister, accompanied by the Postmaster, stared down gravely at her.

"I'm so sorry, Mrs. Quarterman. I have very sad news for you," the Minister began hesitantly, then he told her of the accident on the railway line. He quickly helped Amelia into a chair as she swayed, disbelieving. Her beloved James—gone so suddenly. She would never see him again.

"It can't be so!" she gasped, her husband's last words ringing in her ears: "In a year's time she'll be toddling across the room, bringing me my slippers when I come home from work . . . ."

The next few hours passed in a blur, the silence in the room broken only by the occasional crying of Daisy wanting to be fed. Amelia sat, unseeing, on the sofa, her eyes red and swollen. But news spread quickly in Ealing, and it wasn't long before her brother Henry Dumbleton and his wife Elizabeth arrived at the house, with their daughter Sarah.

Elizabeth put the kettle on the wood stove and set out some teacups, then buttered the home made bread that she had brought with her.

"You need to eat and drink something, Amelia," she urged, placing the food on the table beside her, "you have to keep up your strength for Daisy's sake."

Her neighbour fetched Nellie home from school, and Amelia, numb with grief, took her daughter in her arms.

"Your father has gone to Heaven, Nellie," Amelia gently told her, recounting the tragic accident.

"No! No. I can't believe it," Nellie gasped, cupping her hands over her mouth. Clinging to her mother, she wept bitterly. Only a few hours earlier her father had warned her to be careful in the mist. That awful mist! It was the cause of her father's death. Now he was gone, and she would never see him again. This was even worse than the day Olive had died!

Amelia then sent for her son James Jr. and her daughter Mary (Polly), both apprenticed to a draper in London. Funeral arrangements would have to be made, and a family conference held to discuss the future, to decide how to meet the needs of her family without a husband to support them.

James and Polly arrived by train the next morning, to find their mother in the parlour, in the company of sympathetic members of the Methodist congregation, offering whatever help they could. The news of the accident had shocked the residents of Ealing, as James Quarterman was well known and highly respected.

When the visitors had departed, her son James put a comforting arm around Amelia's shoulders.

"I'll help you in whatever way I can, Mother. When I've finished my apprenticeship I'll be earning some money." With the sudden death of his father, the responsibility of helping to care for his family weighed heavily on the shoulders of the nineteen-year-old.

Polly, looking drawn and older than her twenty-one years, took the grieving Nellie on her lap and held her in a warm embrace, ignoring the tears that splashed across the front of her black dress. Gradually Nellie's tears subsided and Polly dabbed her little sister's face.

"Maybe you can help me a little, Nellie," she suggested softly, "If you wash the tea cups I'll be able to see to Daisy. She needs a clean night gown and jacket."

Being a devout Christian woman, Amelia summoned the strength to gather her family together. "There will be dark days ahead," she told them, "but we'll make ourselves go on living normally. So let's place our trust in God and He will give us strength." With that they held hands and prayed for guidance.

On the day of James' funeral the sun came out between the clouds. Nellie slipped out into the garden and knelt beside the elm tree, where she carefully picked the best of the daffodils, and taking them inside, tied them with a white ribbon.

When James' coffin was carried into the church by the pall-bearers, Nellie's posy of daffodils lay on the lid beside the wreath provided by her family. Tears trickled down her cheeks and splashed onto her dress as she pressed closer to Polly for comfort. With a heavy heart she tried to imagine life without her father, but she could not.

The Minister led the funeral service, with the choir singing "Rock of ages, cleft for me," and at its close the mourners walked to the cemetery nearby, where James was laid to rest.

James Quarterman Jr, as a young man.

CHAPTER 2

GROWING UP IN EALING

During the following weeks help poured in from the congregation, and the Methodist Church assured Amelia that she could remain in the cottage until she was able to arrange alternative accommodation. The Railways, admitting liability for the accident, paid her compensation.

However, Amelia was far from secure financially, so to make ends meet she rented a three storey house at 34 Oxford Street nearby and sub-let the top portion to an elderly lady, Madame Dumont.

Known to the family as Mady, she soon made herself at home, and Amelia was glad of her company as she adjusted to the lonely life of a widow. Having spent her childhood in France and Russia, Mady could tell enthralling tales of life in the land of the Czars.

"When I was young I sped over the snow in a horse drawn sled," she told Nellie, "and we could hear the eerie baying of the wolves in the distance."

Nellie listened, fascinated, as Mady recounted her adventures in France and Russia, and how she trained to become a governess, working in both those countries. At one time she had even been a governess to the children of the Czar of Russia. Later she returned to France and eventually travelled to England to teach the children of an English Lord in the countryside.

Mady spent a great deal of her time caring for baby Daisy, while Amelia cleaned the home and attended to the needs of Nellie. The little girl missed her father, to whom she had been very close, and to add to her sorrow, there was this little baby, usurping the attention that had once been hers as the youngest in the family. Nellie resolved to do something about it.

"Mother," Nellie said to Amelia, "I've spoken to Mrs. Smith up the road, and she offered me ten shillings for Daisy."

Amelia smiled and drew her daughter close to her.

"Having a new baby in the house doesn't make me love you any less, Nellie," she assured her. "Each child has a special place in their mother's heart, no matter how many children there are!"

However, as Daisy grew sturdier by the month, Nellie even began to like her little sister, and sometimes Amelia allowed her to take her in the pram to Ealing Common in the afternoons, accompanied by her fifteen-year-old cousin Sarah. There the two girls played under the shady trees on a huge stretch of grassy parkland, or delighted in splashing their faces in the water bubbling out of the fountain. Donkey rides were also fascinating pastimes on the Common; in fact, all sorts of interesting things happened there.

One sunny afternoon, with Daisy strapped in her pram, the girls parked her beneath a shady tree while they drank from the fountain. Suddenly a movement on the Common attracted Nellie's attention.

"Look," she exclaimed, "A bull—charging straight towards us!"

Sarah turned. "Oh, what'll we do?" she gasped, "What about Daisy?"

Without stopping to reply, Nellie dashed to the pram, tipped it over on its side and took shelter with Sarah behind a clump of bushes. As the "bull" charged past and disappeared into a cluster of trees at the far end of the Common, they burst out laughing.

"A cow!" exploded Nellie. "How silly we are!"

Hastily the girls returned to the indignantly squealing Daisy and tipped her pram upright again.

Life carried on uneventfully in the Quarterman household, with James and Polly visiting the family as often as they could. Eventually, with their apprenticeships in the drapery business completed, (a fact for which Amelia was thankful, as she had to pay for the privilege of them being apprenticed to the draper), James and Polly found employment in London and were able to visit Amelia, Nellie and Daisy on the weekends.

During the following few years Nellie continued attending school in Ealing, and Daisy grew into a happy, healthy little girl.

At the age of seventeen, Nellie as yet had no prospective husband. She would need to find some sort of employment. Amelia called a family conference.

"Nellie," Amelia said gently, "as you know, we are not wealthy, so we will have to find work for you. I have heard of an elderly couple in Brighton who are looking for a companion."

"It would be very pleasant to live beside the sea," suggested Polly.

"Much more pleasant than being a housemaid in Ealing," added James, "and besides, you could come home for weekends quite often."

Amelia watched Nellie's face as the young woman pondered over her future. Eventually Nellie nodded in agreement.

James accompanied Nellie to her new position in Brighton, where she soon settled into the home of the kindly couple, and Amelia began to adjust to life without her young daughter.

Daisy, at the age of six, was alone with Amelia and Mady, while James and Polly were at work. It was natural, therefore, to spend time after school with old Mady, whose collection of delicate china figurines and beautiful ornaments fascinated her. Mady, recalling her experiences as a governess to the children of the Czar of Russia, took time to teach Daisy the Russian alphabet, as well as a few French phrases.

"I shall take you shopping today, Daisy," she informed her one summer afternoon, "as there is something I want to buy for you." With Mady supported by her walking stick and Daisy skipping merrily along the path, they set out for the shops in Ealing.

"What will you buy at the shops, Mady?" Daisy asked, trying to contain her curiosity.

"You'll have to wait and see, Daisy," replied Mady, her eyes twinkling. Then, much to Daisy's delight, Mady bought her a wax doll with delicately painted eyes and mouth and two pink cheeks.

"Oh, she's beautiful. Thank you—thank you, Mady!" Daisy cried, her eyes shining with delight, as she held the doll and rocked it as though it were a baby.

The next few days Mady painstakingly sewed by hand a billowing skirt to cover the doll's long—legged body. Next she stitched some lace around the edge of the skirt.

"Play with your doll as often as you wish, Daisy," Mady said, "but leave it in my bedroom, and never take it into the sun, for it will surely melt."

Daisy obediently adhered to this advice, until one day, when Mady was out, and she was left with time on her hands. The temptation to take the doll outdoors was too strong to resist, and Daisy played happily with the doll beneath the tree. But inevitably the doll was put aside as something else attracted her attention, and when she returned she found, to her dismay, that the sky-blue eyes and pink cheeks had become one, while the delicate little nose tried valiantly to uphold its position.

"Oh, Daisy. What have you done?" exclaimed Mady upon her return, surveying the damage. "We'll have to see whether we can fix your poor doll's pretty face," she said, while her deft fingers gently smoothed the delicate face into position and repainted its features.

On one occasion Mady dressed Daisy in her best Sunday dress of dark blue material with numerous buttons down the front, a warm coat, black leggings and a pleated blue bonnet to cover her long hair, then they walked to the Manor House in Ealing to visit the two spinster ladies, Miss Louisa and Miss Frederica. Daisy enjoyed the walk along the narrow country lane, where the overhanging trees mingled their branches, letting through patches of sunlight, and the bluebells grew in thick clusters alongside the path.

On their arrival the gardener's children opened the large wooden gate to let them into the garden, and Daisy was whisked off to the kitchen to visit the cook, who had a tasty piece of cake for her and for each of the gardener's two children. Watching the servants cleaning the elaborate silverware, she sat wide-eyed in wonder, revelling in the finery about her while she chatted to them as they ate their meal seated in a large hall.

Eventually Daisy was summoned to pay her respects to the spinsters, who presented an awe-inspiring picture. Sitting very erect on their Victorian style chairs, their full-skirted grey dresses billowed around them, with just a glimpse of their white stockings and soft black shoes. Mindful of her manners, Daisy spoke only when spoken to by the ladies, and thanked them for their hospitality when leaving.

"Let's walk past the stable so that I can see the horses, please Mady," Daisy begged on the way home.

After visiting each of the six horses, the stable hands let her see the carriage, and picked her up so that she actually sat on the brown leather seat inside. To her it was a thrilling moment in her life.

"One day, when I'm a lady, I am going to ride in a fine carriage too," Daisy vowed to Mady, "and I shall wear beautiful dresses and shoes—just like Miss Louisa and Miss Frederica. How kind of them to sometimes send their carriage to fetch you, Mady."

"Yes, indeed," agreed Mady with a smile.

Daisy also looked forward to James, Polly and Nellie returning home for the occasional weekend visit, laden with little gifts for her, and on sunny days the family would pack a picnic basket and spend the day on Ealing Common.

During Queen Victoria's Golden Jubilee celebrations in 1887, James and Amelia took Daisy to Walpole Park, which was part of the Manor grounds. It was opened to the public for the day, and each excited child was given a souvenir Jubilee mug of Royal Doulton china and a drink of ginger beer to mark the occasion.

Later the crowd drifted onto the streets of Ealing to await the arrival of Queen Victoria, who would be driven through the town. Having secured a good viewpoint for the family, James settled down with Amelia and Daisy to wait for her appearance.

At last the Queen's horse drawn carriage rounded the corner. The crowd went wild, waving their Union Jack flags and cheering "Hooray," as the Queen's carriage drove slowly by. The Queen lifted a gloved hand and waved to the crowd.

Daisy let out a cry of disappointment. "Where's her crown?" she demanded, "and look—she's wearing an ordinary black dress and no jewellery!" However, despite the plump Queen's unpretentious appearance, she was given a tumultuous welcome, and there was no doubt of the affection of the people for the Monarch.

"If I were the Queen, I would wear a golden crown and a splendid dress of satin and lace, and I would have six white horses to pull my golden carriage," Daisy solemnly announced.

Amelia smiled. "Queen Victoria does not wish to dress in such fine clothes, Daisy," she informed her, "because she is a widow and is still in mourning after the death of her beloved husband, Prince Albert. And besides, the Queen's golden carriage is used for Royal weddings and Coronations."

As Daisy grew older, her remarks and actions were a constant source of surprise to Amelia, causing her to recall James' predictions for the life of his newborn daughter. Daisy certainly did not fit into the mould of a demure Victorian child. She was far more interested in the outside world and was constantly yearning for adventure.

A tomboy by nature, Daisy loved to swing on the creaking garden gate, much to the annoyance of their elderly neighbour, Mrs. Green.

"Your high-spirited daughter needs to be closely controlled, Mrs. Quarterman, otherwise no good will come of her!" she advised Amelia, wagging her finger sagely.

Amelia bristled, but managed to reply politely, "She's still very young, Mrs. Green, and she'll settle down as she grows older."

Daisy's favourite pastime was to climb the large, spreading apple tree in the back garden. There, nestling in the branches, she could dream of adventures in far off lands.

Amelia, shaking her head at such unladylike practices, wondered if her little daughter would ever grow up to be a lady. After all, she pondered, a nine-year-old should spend her time in more useful pursuits, such as needlework.

"Daisy," she said one sunny afternoon, "you're far too tomboyish. Leave the trees for boys to climb. After all, you are a girl, you know, and girls shouldn't do such things. If you've nothing better to do, why don't you take a book into the garden and read it? Climbing trees is a waste of time, but you may learn something useful from a book."

Daisy selected a book of adventure and settled down on the garden bench to read it. Above her, perched high up in the apple tree, a pair of starlings chattered, as if calling to her. For a moment she was tempted to join them. It would take only a minute to climb up to the top of the tree—and what a lovely view she would have from its strong branches. Then she sighed as she thought of her mother's words. How dull it was to be a girl!

Her gaze wandered from the top of the tree to the high wall separating their garden from the neighbour's, and all at once an impish grin lit up her face. Her mother had told her not to climb trees, but she hadn't said anything about climbing garden walls! Searching for a foothold in the wall she discovered a loose brick, which she deftly pulled out. Then, climbing laboriously to the top, with the book tucked into the bodice of her dress, she settled down on the narrow ledge to gaze at the interesting row of back gardens stretching as far as the main street.

She became absorbed in her book once more, as the pages yielded exciting tales about life in far-off Africa, where lions wandered in the dense bush and monkeys chattered in the trees. Her friend's father, who had been a missionary in Africa, had often told them enthralling tales about his encounters with wild animals and of the dark skinned boys and girls who lived in thatched huts and kept their cattle in kraals, or enclosures.

Daisy shifted her position ever so slightly as the wall began to feel hard and uncomfortable.

Suddenly, without warning, she toppled backwards over the wall. With an ear splitting yell she disappeared into the neighbour's rubbish bin.

Amelia and Mrs. Green rushed out at the sound of Daisy's yell. To their surprise a pair of stockinged legs thrashed wildly above the rim of the rubbish bin. Then, amidst a cloud of dust and dirt, emerged a wriggling, bedraggled figure, loudly bewailing her fate!

"Oh, Daisy," Amelia cried in exasperation, "what will you do next?"

Daisy coughed and spluttered, shaking her dress vainly to get rid of the dirt. She didn't dare look at Mrs. Green, standing in her kitchen doorway with her hands on her hips.

Suppressing an amused smile, Amelia marched her daughter into the house. Placing the tin bath beside the coal stove in the kitchen, she filled it with hot water from the pot and the kettle on the stove, adding enough cold water to make it pleasantly warm. Daisy sank gratefully into the large bath, washing herself vigorously while Amelia poured warm water over her hair. After a soak in the bath and a change of clothing she was none the worse for her experience.

Daisy Quarterman as a little girl in Ealing.

CHAPTER 3

AMELIA JOINS THE SALVATION ARMY

By the time Daisy had turned nine years old, Amelia and Polly had become interested in the work of William Booth, a former Methodist minister in the cathedral city of Salisbury, who, for many years, had been a champion of the poor.

While walking through the slums of London one evening in 1865, Booth gazed aghast at the hungry children, drunken men and women and their squalid homes. Pity stirred within him for these wretched people, with no hope of a better life. Above all, he was concerned for their souls. These ragged, filthy people would never set foot in one of the established churches; indeed, should they dare to do so, they would have to sit in the few rows reserved for them at the back of the church. God's word was for all—for these people too—and yet their spiritual welfare was being neglected.

Soon Booth's tall, bearded figure became a familiar sight, preaching on street corners, in dilapidated buildings or anywhere else where he could gather a few people together. His courageous wife Catherine encouraged him in his work and even preached herself, despite the responsibility of rearing seven children.

Gathering some Christian workers together, he founded the East London Christian Revival Society, its aim being to take part in evangelical and social welfare work in London's slum areas.

Many difficult years followed for the Booth family. Living among the poor, and without a steady income, they knew hardship and discomfort; yet so dedicated were they to their cause that they carried on against all their setbacks. They expanded their work wherever they could, and changed their name twice: firstly to the East London Christian Mission, and then, recognizing the increasing area of their influence, simply to the Christian Mission, which was established in 1869. Their work continued to grow rapidly, and in 1878 it was reorganized along its present quasi-military lines, under the new name of The Salvation Army, with Booth accorded the title of General. Military ranks and titles were given to the Officers and members of the organization according to their duties.

At first Londoners did not take kindly to this new organization. Its members were often faced with derision and the street urchins pelted them with rotten vegetables as they marched through the streets near the market place of Covent Garden.

Eventually Charles Fry, a builder and leader of the Salisbury Methodist Church choir, offered Booth the services of himself and his three sons. Their intention was to provide Booth's followers with bodyguards while they preached. By coincidence the Fry family had brass instruments, and offered to bring them along to accompany those preaching. When it was found that the music attracted people and also had a calming effect, Booth decided to make use of music in the services. In this way the Salvation Army bands unwittingly came into being.

Booth went about his work with a fiery determination. His followers gathered on street corners with their brass bands, preaching to anyone who would listen. Slowly his work began to bear fruit. Drunkards were converted and joined the Salvation Army, helping to swell their ranks.

Amelia, always a champion of the poor, became interested in the work of William and Catherine Booth and helped the Salvation Army by collecting used clothing from her friends and neighbours. She was soon good friends with the Booth family, and eventually left the Methodist Church and joined the Salvation Army in 1889. Three years earlier, Polly had become so interested in the movement that she had become an Officer in the Salvation Army, stationed in Shepherd's Bush, a western suburb of London.

Daisy looked forward to Sundays, when Amelia took her to the Clapton Congress Hall in London, the Training Centre for Salvation Army Officers, that was always full for the Sunday services. Unorthodox in their methods of running the service, the clapping of hands, playing of tambourines and a wave offering, where everyone waved their best handkerchiefs in time to the music, were common practices.

One service made an indelible impression on the young girl's mind. It was an international congress, and when the demonstration began, representatives from various countries came forward, each dressed in their national costume, while the massed band played stirring music. This tableau depicted the rapid growth of the Salvation Army in various parts of the world.

Daisy sat wide-eyed with excitement at the sight of the spectacle. As those taking part came towards the platform they saluted the large yellow, red and blue flag which was held upright, and she noticed that scores of little children in the congregation were waving handkerchiefs with the same colours as the flag.

"Oh, I wish I had a handkerchief like that," she exclaimed to James, who had accompanied them. "Please buy me one and bring it home over the weekend. Please, James!"

When at last the coveted handkerchief arrived, Daisy promptly fastened it to a stick and marched around the garden, lustily singing: "Onward Christian soldiers, marching as to war," her only audience being the family cat, perched lazily on the garden wall.

The Salvationists marching in the streets also intrigued Daisy, and it was not long before she begged to accompany Polly to one of her meetings in London.

"The hooligans in the streets are rough, Daisy," Polly warned, "so you'll have to stay close by me."

"Oh, I will, I will!" Daisy promised breathlessly, "Say I can go with you on Sunday."

Polly looked down at her eager little sister, her eyes shining in anticipation. How could she refuse?

"Very well," Polly agreed reluctantly, "but remember, you'll have to be very careful."

That Sunday Daisy marched proudly with her sister through the slums of Bethnal Green, led by the bandsmen playing their drums and trumpets. At the sound of their cheerful tunes Daisy wanted to skip with joy, and only by an effort of will refrained from doing so.

The hooligans turned up, as usual, in full force.

"Yer fink yer better than us, do yer?" one unkempt young man hollered, "Just because yer wearing them fancy uniforms. Well, take that!"

Vegetable stalks swished about their legs and rotten tomatoes plopped around them.

"Don't be afraid, Daisy—just keep on walking," Polly advised, drawing Daisy closer to her. Suddenly, with a cry of pain, Daisy pressed her hand over her eye. Someone had thrown a lemon at her!

"What horrible people," she cried, "they could have blinded me."

Polly paused to assess the damage and put a comforting arm across her shoulders.

"But they haven't," she said, "although your eyelid and cheek look bruised. Never mind. All the more reason why they need to be saved, Daisy. Don't let these hooligans put you off. We'll win in the end, you'll see!"

Daisy pursed her lips as the tears ran down her cheeks.

"Suppose so," she said, sounding somewhat unconvinced.

Later, in the train going home, Daisy cupped her hand over her still smarting eye.

"We'll fight the good fight. We'll show them!" she exclaimed.

To which Polly responded with a fervent "Amen!"

Mary (Polly) Quarterman, aged thirty-two.

CHAPTER 4

AT THE CROSSROADS

Since Nellie's visits home from Brighton were very infrequent and Polly was busily engaged in her work with the Salvation Army, Daisy had no elder sister to restrain her boisterous behaviour. She became livelier than ever, much to the disapproval of Amelia's friends, who would shake their heads and wonder what on earth would ever become of her. After all, a twelve-year-old girl should start behaving like a young lady.

Schoolwork, thought Daisy, was a pastime that unfortunately had to be endured, affording little enjoyment; particularly as her school teacher placed great emphasis on good deportment. She was not averse to giving a child a sharp tap between the shoulder blades should she be caught slouching over her desk.

Even Sister Clarke, who, after her hospital duties, gave lessons in first aid, nutrition and health care in her class called Band of Love, was not immune to Daisy's fun-loving antics. While the Sister was trying to teach the girls, Daisy began to scheme a mischievous prank.

Sister Clarke's favourite subject was botany, which she expounded at length in her squeaky, high pitched voice, and when she arrived one day carrying a large, juicy carrot, the class took one look at Daisy's face to note her reaction. Trying to suppress the grin that was spreading rapidly across her face, and with a glint in her eye, she awaited her opportunity.

Sister Clarke glared suspiciously at the grinning girls.

"There's nothing funny about a carrot," she squeaked, "and after I have told you all about it you will realize what an important vegetable it is."

She settled down in her chair, placing her carrot on the chair behind her, and opened her notebook to read from her carefully prepared notes.

So absorbed was the short-sighted Sister that she did not notice Daisy slip from her chair and creep up behind her on the platform. In a flash Daisy pinned the carrot stalks into the folds of Sister Clarke's veil, then tiptoed hastily back to her seat at the end of the semi circle.

"Now, girls," said Sister Clarke, closing her book, "I hope you have learned something about the nutritional value of the carrot tonight."

She stretched out her hand to the seat behind her, then stared in disbelief at the empty chair. There was no carrot in sight. She searched the floor, but that proved equally fruitless. Pointing an accusing finger at the half-circle of giggling girls, she shrilled: "Someone has taken my carrot. Give it back at once!" And with every indignant bob of her head the carrot bounced at the end of her long veil.

Presently the direction of the girls' gaze indicated where she should look, but nobody would say who had pinned it there. Thoroughly mortified, and mumbling to herself, Sister Clarke marched out of the room, leaving the girls to their fit of uncontrollable giggles.

The next day Amelia had a visit from the still troubled Sister Clarke.

"Oh, Mrs. Quarterman," she sighed, "I feel I can no longer go on with the Band of Love. Such a dreadful thing happened last night!" Amelia listened sympathetically as Sister Clarke recounted the events of the previous night.

"Do you have any idea who did it?" enquired Amelia, casting a suspicious glance at Daisy, who was beating a hasty retreat past the parlour door.

"None whatsoever," Sister Clarke replied, "but whoever did it seems to have a great deal of influence over the others—nobody would tell me who did it!"

"When Sister Clarke said that," Daisy recounted later to her friends, "Mother looked suspiciously at me, so I disappeared fast!" But she didn't tell them what Amelia said when she eventually caught up with her.

Having a happy, cheerful disposition, Daisy attracted a large circle of friends who always looked to her for leadership, and as the years went by this ability to lead others became more apparent in the young girl. Possessing a lively sense of humour, she would sometimes set the girls giggling during the service, much to the Sergeant-Major's disapproval.

One Sunday after the service, while tripping cheerfully down the stairs from the hall, she accidentally trod on the hem of the gown worn by a lady walking ahead of her. To her mortification, the woman turned around and indignantly flipped her ears!

Eventually the Sergeant-Major decided it was time to have a word with her.

"You are fourteen years old now, Daisy," he said, "and you're no longer a child. I suppose you do realize, don't you, that you have a very strong influence over your friends?"

"Influence over them?" Daisy echoed, puzzled. "I don't influence them at all. They do just as they wish."

"No, Daisy," corrected the Sergeant-Major, "not as they wish—as you wish!"

Daisy was silent as she turned this new thought over in her mind. A strong influence over them? Yes, maybe it was so. It was strange, she thought, how she had never noticed this before.

"Don't you realize," he continued, "that this influence you are able to wield over others has been given to you for a purpose? Are you going to use it for the good of others, or will you influence your friends to live empty, foolish lives? You could lead your friends to Heaven—or you could lead them straight to Hell!"

For once Daisy was at a loss for words. Influence—was this a gift from God? If so, how was she going to use it?

Daisy looked up earnestly at the Sergeant-Major.

"I'll think about what you have said," she promised, as she made her departure.

For the next few days Daisy was subdued. The Sergeant-Major's words kept coming to mind. Slowly she began to realize that although she had been brought up in a Christian home, surrounded by love and prayers, she had not yet given her life wholeheartedly to God. For the first time in her young life she began to think deeply about spiritual matters, but although she could talk freely about other subjects, religion to her was a very personal matter, which she never discussed with anyone.

During the busy time before Christmas, the Quarterman family made their customary arrangements to hold a party on Boxing Day for the poorest children in the Corps. For weeks Daisy had been saving her pocket money to buy small presents and crackers for the children, while Amelia set about baking large quantities of mince pies and shortbread for the party.

"You will come too, won't you Gertie?" Daisy asked her best friend. "We'll have such a lovely party."

With the invitation accepted the girls parted company, but although Daisy was absorbed in her plans for the party, there was a frown on her usually sunny face as she kissed her mother goodnight and went to her room.

Deep down within her heart she knew that she was not truly converted, and this she longed to be. She was looked up to in the Corps and was popular with the Juniors. No doubt, thought Daisy, they would be very surprised if she were to confess that although she had been brought up in a religious home, she had not yet given her life completely and without reservation to the Lord.

Christmas Day came and went, but despite the happy day she had spent with her family, her heart was heavy. The Sergeant-Major's words kept coming to mind: "You could lead your friends to Heaven—or you could lead them straight to Hell."

The enormous responsibility resting upon her young shoulders was frightening. She did not wish to lead her friends astray—yet how could she lead them to God if she herself had not found the way to Him?

On Boxing Day Daisy and Gertie worked all morning, preparing for the arrival of their guests. That afternoon the sitting room was full to overflowing with sparkling-eyed children enjoying the feast, as for many of them, this was the first taste of Christmas fare in which they had shared. The plates were rapidly cleared of their contents and peals of merry laughter drifted up to Amelia as she rested in her bedroom.

When the guests and Gertie had departed, Daisy joined her mother on the bed and laid her tired head on her shoulder. Unaware that Daisy had a very heavy heart, she cuddled her daughter as they talked about the party and how much the children had enjoyed it.

But all through that evening the words rang in Daisy's ears: "You are not right with God!" and she was finding it difficult to fight against conviction.

On New Year's Eve Daisy had made up her mind.

"I'm going to the Watch Night Service tonight," she told Gertie, "and I'm going to get right with God! There's so much in my life that needs to be put right."

Gertie gasped in astonishment. "But my mother says you're so good, and I've always thought you were the best girl in the Corps."

"Well, I'm not," replied Daisy gloomily. "Sergeant—Major says I have a strong influence over you girls, and that I could lead you straight to Heaven—or to Hell. I can't lead you to Heaven when I don't know the way myself."

That New Year's Eve the hall was packed with people at the Watch Night Service, for it was customary to see the New Year in on their knees, with a prayer of dedication for the year to come.

Addressing the meeting, the Captain pointed out that it was all very well to make New Year resolutions, but that they could not always be kept unless those making them changed their ways and committed their lives to God.

Daisy felt strangely moved at his words. Was God trying to tell her that without Him at her side all her efforts would be in vain? Then she kept thinking of a verse from the Bible: "I can do all things through Christ who strengtheneth me."

As was customary at the Watch Night Service, the Captain asked all those who wished to dedicate their lives to God to come forward. Without hesitation Daisy stood up and walked towards the wooden Mercy Seat at the front of the hall, where other Salvationists were beginning to kneel in prayer. As the last moments of the old year ticked away, she realized with a sense of wonder and joy that her sins had gone too, into the sea of God's forgiveness. Although her face was tear-stained as she rose to her feet, her heart was happy as she joined the congregation in singing those beautiful words of consecration:

"Take my life, and let it be, consecrated Lord to Thee."

And Daisy vowed then that she would spend the rest of her life in the service of the Master. Something within her asked: "Your life as an Officer in the Salvation Army?"

"Yes, Lord," she answered as she walked beneath the lamp lights on the snow covered streets on her way home, "Take my life for anything or anywhere."

From that day onwards there was a marked change in Daisy. Although still as vivacious as ever, childish frivolity no longer appealed to her. It was as though she had taken the final step from childhood to young womanhood, leaving behind the fascinations of yesteryear as she sought for the true values of life.

Amelia Quarterman

CHAPTER 5

A DIFFICULT DECISION

Daisy was a little nervous as she approached the Sergeant-Major and offered her services as a helper with the Juniors; for although she was very fond of children, her youth and inexperience made her feel inadequate for the task. However, her conviction that God had called her into His service was so strong that she was able to overcome her fear.

The Sergeant-Major was delighted with her decision.

"I'm glad you've decided to help in the Corps, Daisy. You can be a helper in a Company of poor children. Many of them are rough and dirty, and you'll need endless patience with them. Do you think you can handle it?" he asked.

"Yes, I'm ready," Daisy smiled, and it was not long before she had joined the staff in the Company and was soon making friends with the little street urchins who attended the meetings. Using her boundless energy to work among them, she found a deep satisfaction that she had never before experienced.

Life was full and interesting for the young girl now. A series of lectures followed, which she had to attend to qualify for Senior Soldiership, and at the age of 16 she enrolled as a Soldier in the Salvation Army, along with thirty-three others, at a special meeting.

Thereafter her responsibilities increased, and under the guidance of the Sergeant-Major, she learned to control her rough little charges.

A year later the Sergeant-Major called her into his office.

"I want to share some news with you, Daisy," he said, "I'm leaving this neighbourhood to get married, and I'll be taking up a position elsewhere. You'll have a new Sergeant-Major here."

Daisy looked at him in dismay. She had come to respect this forthright man and to seek his advice. Now he would be leaving. Would his replacement be so understanding and so cooperative? A good leader could make such a difference to those who worked under him.

His next words gave her a start.

"I'm thinking of proposing you as Young People's Sergeant-Major, Daisy. Will you take on the job?"

Daisy stared at him in amazement.

"Me?" she gasped, turning over in her mind the seriousness of the responsibility. Would she be able to cope with such an undertaking? Then she thought of all the youngsters under her care. She couldn't let them down.

"Yes," she said slowly, "I'll do my best."

"Good," he beamed, "I knew you'd agree to do the job. I expect great things of you, Daisy. With the influence you are able to wield over others, you could become a power for good in the Young People's Corps."

When Daisy arrived home, she sought Amelia's advice.

"I'm proud of the decision you've made, Daisy," Amelia said, giving her daughter a hug. "You'll gain valuable experience—and that will stand you in good stead in the years to come."

One hundred and fifty children attended the Sunday afternoon meetings, mainly to seek entertainment. As many of them were rough and ignorant, they were the despair of the Company Guards, who found it difficult to control them.

Daisy thoughtfully viewed the situation and approached her friends.

"These children haven't had much education," she told them, "and the lessons we are giving them are sometimes way above their heads. We're not here to teach them choruses and entertain them with music; we have to teach them the word of God."

Looking around at the group of young women, she could see that they were considering what she had been telling them.

"We need to simplify the lessons and present them in a way that the children can understand," went on Daisy, "and we can't teach them properly unless we have enough efficient Company Guards."

Pausing long enough to allow her words to make an impression on them, she then issued them with a challenge.

"Here's your chance to do something for the Corps. How about volunteering as Company Guards?"

She watched with gratitude as each one of her friends—those same ones who had encouraged her to get into mischief in their childhood—offered to help her. The Sergeant-Major was right. She did have a certain amount of influence over them.

Daisy introduced preparation meetings to simplify the lessons and make them more interesting. These lessons were usually held in Amelia's kitchen, with Daisy perched on the kitchen table, swinging her legs, while she led the discussions. Invariably kind-hearted Amelia appeared with hot chocolate and biscuits after the meeting, "to warm you girls up before you go out into the cold night air."

It was not long before their work started to bear fruit. With more Company Guards to work with the children, they behaved better and many were eager to learn.

Within months it was obvious that their Company Guards were among the best in the district, and it was then that Daisy issued them with a new challenge.

"If a child stays away from the meetings," suggested Daisy, "then there must be a reason for it. Maybe they are ill, or they feel that they are not important enough to be missed. We ought to find out the reason."

Pausing long enough to let her words sink in, she went on: "And the only way to find out," she suggested, "is to visit them in their homes."

There was an audible gasp as the girls shifted uneasily in their seats.

"Many of those children live in rough areas, Daisy," Gertie reminded her, "and I'm not sure just how safe it will be for us to go there."

"Then I suggest that you go in twos, and only in daylight," said Daisy. "When someone answers the doorbell you can stand at the door and deliver your message—you don't need to go inside the house."

After two months of visiting the families, they found that attendance at the Sunday afternoon meetings had increased, and the Company Guards were getting to know the families and gaining their confidence.

By the time Daisy turned eighteen she was a mature young woman, with wide, thoughtful eyes and dimpled cheeks. Still bubbling over with life and laughter, she attracted a large circle of friends.

Life was interesting and exciting. Seated at her bedroom window, she watched the carriages go by in the early evenings, carrying elegantly dressed ladies and gentlemen to the Opera House, and she would dream of the day when she too would be able to taste the pleasures of life.

And yet, there seemed to be a persistent, small voice inside her asking: Will you give your life in unselfish service to others as a Salvation Army Officer? No, no, I can't, she thought to herself, I haven't had the experiences of life that I really want to enjoy before I settle down. Besides, I can't leave Mother all alone. Someone has to care for her, and she'd be lonely if I were to be sent to some other town. And I am doing lots of work for the Army right here in Ealing.

But the still, small voice persisted, tormenting her night and day. Could she leave her mother? Yes, she could if she really wanted to. Her mother was still capable of caring for herself, and Polly, now a Salvation Army Ensign working among the poor in the Piccadilly area of London, would be able to visit Mother frequently.

While still in this uncertain frame of mind she attended a Good Friday meeting conducted by the Army's founder, William Booth, in the Congress Hall in London. Booth's tall, erect figure, flowing beard and piercing eyes made an impressive figure as he spoke in his usual, forthright manner. Listening intently, Daisy felt her doubts disappear as she made her decision. This is the road for me—and I will follow it, she thought.

At first she did not tell Amelia of her secret conviction that God had called her to higher service. How dismayed her mother would be if she were left to live out her old age all alone. Kneeling beside her bed that night, she prayed earnestly for God's guidance.

Soon afterwards a Young People's Council meeting was held, to appeal to young people to come forward and volunteer as Officers in the Army. Yet Daisy still held back, even though she knew what she wanted to do.

As young people all around her got up and went forward to volunteer for service, she sat motionless. Would she be doing the right thing by offering her services, if it meant leaving her mother? Then slowly the thought came to her: Place your trust in God. He will open up the way. Daisy was the hundredth person to go forward and offer her services on that memorable day.

Daisy Quarterman, aged eighteen.

CHAPTER 6

DAISY'S CAREER BEGINS

Amelia noticed a change in Daisy the moment she walked into the house, on her return from the meeting. Her sparkling eyes and shining face told her that her daughter was about to announce something of importance.

"I've offered to become an Officer in the Army, Mother," Daisy said breathlessly, hugging her mother as she spoke.

Amelia's heart sank. First Polly—and now Daisy. How could she face a lonely life without her: this loving child born so late in life who had proved to be such a blessed ray of sunshine? God was indeed asking a great sacrifice from her.

Yet even as these thoughts flashed through her mind she knew that if God had called her daughter to service, she should not stand in her way. She could feel Daisy's eyes scanning her face, awaiting her reaction. She forced herself to smile, although her heart was heavy.

"If God has called you, then you must go, Daisy," she said slowly. "Besides, when I was your age I too felt the call to do missionary work—but somehow I never went. Now you can go in my place."

"Mother, you know what that means, don't you? I'll have to leave you and go to live in the Training Home in Clapton," Daisy reminded her. "Will you be able to cope without me?"

"Yes, my child, I'll manage," Amelia smiled, "and besides, you can come home often to visit me."

Daisy's farewell social was attended by all her friends, young and old, many of whom found it hard to believe that this enthusiastic young candidate offering her services to the Salvation Army as an Officer was the same girl who had played so many mischievous pranks in her early childhood.

Life at the Clapton Training Home proved to be an interesting experience. Accommodating about one hundred women and two hundred men, the rambling old building was a constant hub of activity. The Cadets, as the newcomers were called, had to do their share of the chores, including scrubbing floors, washing clothes and washing dishes. In fact, they were trained to be self-reliant to prepare them for any difficult situation they might meet when they were eventually sent out as missionaries.

Every Sunday the Cadets went out in small groups with the Army Officers to preach in the slums of London. Daisy disliked these excursions immensely. The dirty streets and run-down houses appalled her, yet she felt compassion when she saw the poverty, neglect and ignorance with which they came in contact. The fact that some of the Army Officers actually lived among the people amazed her.

One Sunday a group of trainees was sent to Bethnal Green, a suburb of London, accompanied by a small brass band. Marching through the streets, they were suddenly confronted by a group of ragged street urchins.

"What yer doing here?" they yelled, pelting the Cadets with rotten vegetables. Daisy's heart pounded, remembering that incident many years ago when she had marched with Polly and had been subjected to the same kind of attack.

I'll place my faith in the Lord, she thought, and marched more resolutely than before, singing loudly when the group stopped at a street corner to hold an open-air service. Although faced with ridicule, their leader calmly delivered his message of salvation through Jesus

Christ. In time Daisy became accustomed to this type of behaviour, and accepted it as an inevitable part of their task.

However, their training had its more pleasant occasions. Once a month the Cadets attended a service at the Congress Hall where four hundred people could be seated, and the outstanding band and an inspiring message from the preacher renewed Daisy's spirit and resolve.

Another welcome diversion was their free afternoon each week, when they could go home to visit their families. Amelia looked forward to these visits, for although Polly had been sent home to recuperate and rest after working too hard in the slums of London, she missed the cheerful company of her younger daughter.

Daisy also looked forward to these weekly chats with her mother, for there was always so much to tell her about her experiences, and she invariably returned to the College with an appetising tuck box.

By 1896 the Salvation Army had expanded rapidly, with mission stations established in many countries, and the need was felt for more missionaries to help with the work. Toward the end of the Cadets' training, the Commissioner, who had recently returned from a visit to South Africa, called the Cadets to a special meeting.

"The Army is already established in South Africa," he told them, "but there is still a great need for many more men and women who are prepared to face the hardships of life in a country among people whose customs are foreign to their own. There is a large population of settlers from Holland, France, Germany, England and other countries," he went on, "many of whom emigrated there as long ago as 1652. There is an even larger population of black people as well as people who are descendants of mixed marriages between black and white residents.

Looking around the room at the faces of the young Cadets, he issued a challenge.

"The Territorial Commander in South Africa has requested the help of fifty volunteers. Would you be prepared to offer your services?"

The stories Gertie's father had told her many years ago about life in Africa flashed through Daisy's mind. As a child her interest in missionary work had been stirred; now, listening to the words of the Commissioner, she knew without doubt that this was the way she wanted to spend her life. She raised her hand, along with many others, and with an air of excitement left the meeting and immediately wrote to Amelia.

Amelia's hands trembled as she read Daisy's letter. Africa! How could she allow her young daughter to go to a strange land far away? She could be away for many years—or maybe never come back! The mere thought filled her with dread. And yet she knew how interested Daisy had always been in missionary work. Being a sincere Christian woman, she felt she could not stand in Daisy's way.

When Polly heard the news, however, she was adamant.

"Daisy's too young and inexperienced to do such an arduous job," she exclaimed. Amelia's friends were equally aghast; but Amelia went down on her knees and took her problem to God.

In the meantime, Daisy learned, to her great disappointment, that double the number of Cadets needed had volunteered, and her services would not be required after all. Her dreams of working with the white settlers as well as the dark-skinned little African girls and boys faded. Well, at least, she comforted herself, her mother would be happy that she would not be going away.

During the next few days she set about her studies with a new determination. It was no use fretting about disappointments, she decided, and besides, there was plenty of work for her to do in her own country.

While in this frame of mind she was down on her hands and knees scrubbing the passage floor when Polly and James came to visit her. Putting aside her scrubbing brush, she wiped her hands on her apron and went downstairs to speak to them.

"I've a letter from Mother for you, Daisy," Polly said, handing the letter into her sister's outstretched hand, "and I hope you've changed your mind about volunteering for mission work in South Africa. You're far too young for such a task."

Daisy sighed, wishing that for once her older sister wouldn't be quite so protective.

"I'm not needed, anyway," she said ruefully, "because there were more volunteers than were needed. So at least Mother will be pleased that I'll no longer be going."

"Well, that's a relief," Polly exclaimed and James nodded in agreement.

"Would you like to come out with us today?" James enquired.

"No, thank you. I can't. It's my turn to help with the cleaning," Daisy replied.

Bidding her brother and sister farewell, Daisy slipped the letter into her pocket, and went on with her task.

I'll read my letter in peace when my work is done, she thought, and was busy scrubbing when she heard a step behind her. It was her friend Jessie, her face shining with excitement.

"Are you ready to go to Africa, Daisy?" she asked.

Daisy stopped scrubbing and stared at her in surprise.

"What makes you ask?"

"Well, the Commissioner wants to speak to you in his office, and I've heard that a lot of volunteers have dropped out."

Daisy leaped up. "No! You don't mean . . ."

"That you've got a better chance of going now? Yes!" and Jessie sped off down the passage.

Daisy's heart began to pound. Could it be true? Then suddenly remembering her mother's letter in her pocket, she tore it open and read it as she hurried down the passage.

I have prayed about your decision, Daisy. If you're given the opportunity of going to South Africa, take it, her mother had written.

Amazed at the good news, just when she needed it most, she knocked at the Commissioner's door, hurriedly smoothing her hair and straightening her apron.

The Commissioner invited her into his office, pointing to a chair on the other side of his desk.

"Please be seated, Cadet Quarterman," he said, as he flipped over the pages of a file before him. Then he looked up with a smile.

"Are you ready to go to South Africa, Cadet Quarterman?" he asked.

So it was true! Her face lit up.

"Oh yes, yes. I'm ready and willing!" she cried. How opportune her mother's letter had been.

During the following weeks the Cadets were subjected to various tests, including a medical examination. It was then that the doctor discovered a patch on Daisy's lung, indicating some sort of infection.

"You're making a wise decision," the doctor told her, "moving to a country with plenty of sunshine. Your health will deteriorate if you stay in England. Here you'll be expected to work in all sorts of unpleasant weather; but in South Africa your health should improve. That country has a drier, warmer climate."

The following weeks sped by as the nineteen young women who had volunteered to go to South Africa prepared for their journey. There was much to be done and much to learn about what to expect in a country so different from their own.

Amelia set about the task of equipping her daughter for the sea voyage. She bought her a warm travelling rug and a chest protector made of chamois leather to protect her from the cold. Then, painstakingly she stitched in between the folds of the chest protector a number of half crown coins "in case of need." Daisy, realizing the sacrifice it must have been for her mother, appreciated this gesture all the more.

A farewell social was arranged for the Cadets and a Captain from the educational section of the Clapton Training College, who would escort the young women to South Africa.

The *Tintagel Castle*, the ship on which the Cadets would be sailing, was to leave from Tilbury Docks, London, on December 4th, 1896. The voyage, with a brief stop at Las Palmas, would last 23 days, and was due to end in Cape Town on the 27th December.

At last the long awaited day arrived. Amelia, James, Polly and Nellie joined the throng of relatives and friends of the Cadets on the quayside, at Tilbury, London, where the *Tintagel Castle* was docked. Several Officers were present to see them off on their journey, while the Salvation Army band played some lively tunes and porters dashed about busily moving luggage and supplies to be loaded onto the ship.

James, looking down at his excited young sister, thought of the day when, many years ago, he had given her the coveted little Salvation Army handkerchief, which she had converted into a flag. She had walked under it, loudly singing "Onward Christian Soldiers, marching as to war," and now here she was, marching to another country, to play her part in the war against sin.

Even Gertie was there to bid farewell to her best friend. Huddled beneath her thick shawl to protect her from the cold December weather, she stood there forlornly, trying not to cry.

"You will write to me, Gertie, won't you? And please keep in touch with Mother." Daisy said, giving her friend a warm farewell hug.

Daisy, dressed smartly in her immaculate uniform of fitted navy blue jacket, ankle length skirt and wide brimmed blue bonnet, embraced each of her family members, the tears streaming down her cheeks. She was leaving her beloved family behind in England, while she set sail for an unknown land.

Amelia held her youngest daughter close for one last time, trying to hold onto the moment forever. Her beloved Daisy, looking so young and vulnerable, was leaving her. Would she ever see her again? South Africa was such a long way from England. At that moment she felt that the sacrifice she was making was almost too great to bear.

Then it was time to board the *Tintagel Castle*. As the Cadets lined up and walked up the gangway to the ship, the Salvation Army band played a rousing tune of encouragement.

The young Cadets joined the other passengers crowding onto the deck to wave to those below on the quay. Dock workers moved the last gangway ashore, the ropes securing the vessel to the quayside were thrown off and the ship's whistle sounded. The stately liner glided slowly away as it began its long journey to South Africa.

Daisy, standing silently at the railing, watched the figures of her family grow smaller in the ever—widening distance as they waved farewell to her. How long would it be before she was reunited with her dear family? Slightly built for her eighteen years, she looked, and felt at that moment, completely alone. Then, with mixed emotions, she turned and walked through the doorway into the warmth of the ship. For the nineteen young missionaries, the adventure of their lives was about to begin.

CHAPTER 7

THE VOYAGE TO SOUTH AFRICA

Seated at a window in the ship's sitting room, Daisy gazed silently as the green hills and cottages scattered along the shore disappeared slowly from sight as the *Tintagel Castle* made its way out to the open sea. She was leaving England, the country she knew and loved, bound for a strange country with settlers from many different lands, as well as many dark-skinned African people, all living in a land of sunshine.

The sheltered waters of the River Thames gave way to the gentle rolling of the sea as the ship headed towards the English Channel. They would be passing Margate, then rounding the tip of the North Foreland. Daisy wondered whether they would see the white cliffs of Dover, but that question was answered as wisps of mist drifted past the ship, making it difficult to see the shore.

"Well, I suppose we ought to make ourselves comfortable in our cabins," Daisy remarked to her friend Jessie, and found, to her surprise, that the feeling of excitement at what lay ahead in their lives began to lift her spirits.

The *Tintagel Castle*, having been built earlier that year, was regarded as a modern, comfortable ship, with a length of over four hundred and twenty feet and a service speed of 15 knots. Although driven by steam, it also had four large masts and sails to take advantage of favourable winds to speed it on its journey. Their cabin, designed for four passengers, had two upper bunks and two lower ones, with storage space for their possessions. After unpacking they tidied themselves and went upstairs to their first dinner aboard.

The Cadets found themselves the source of interest among the passengers, many of whom were young men headed for the gold mines and diamond fields of South Africa. They too were travelling to an unknown land, leaving behind their families as they set out to find employment.

The industrial revolution in Britain had caused massive unemployment, resulting in thousands of people leaving their homeland, bound for Canada, Australia, New Zealand and South Africa in search of a better life. Some of them had left for hotter climates in the hope of a cure for chest ailments, and in fact, some ships were called the "invalid ships" because of the poor state of health of the passengers.

Daisy, looking around her at the passengers, noted with relief that they appeared to be fairly healthy, although some were somewhat rough and boisterous.

That evening the ship, well into the English Channel, encountered fierce gales and rough seas, tossing it about and forcing the passengers to head for their bunks to ride out the storm. December is usually a bad month for a passage through the English Channel, but the *Tintagel Castle's* voyage proved to be an exceptionally rough one. For days all the Cadets were confined to their beds with sea sickness, with the worst part of the voyage being the Bay of Biscay three days after their departure.

"Will this tossing about ever stop?" enquired Jessie plaintively, trying vainly to stand upright in the cabin. She lurched across the room and then turned back to her lower bunk, where she remained for the rest of the day.

"I believe we will be reaching the Spanish island of Tenerife soon," said Daisy hopefully,

"and by then we should be feeling better."

The sea gradually became calmer, and by the fifth day in the early morning, land was sighted. The weary Cadets straggled upstairs to the deck, and at once their spirits lifted as Tenerife, bathed in sunlight, appeared before them. Its high, snow capped mountain peak towered above the clouds that drifted down to the base of the mountain, around which a small settlement of cottages nestled among palm trees on the rocky shore.

"I wish we could explore that island," remarked Daisy, gazing longingly at the interesting little settlement. However, the ship continued on its journey between the Canary Islands off the coast of Morocco, and at noon arrived at Las Palmas, a larger Spanish island, where it dropped anchor in the bay.

This island was even more beautiful than Tenerife. Numerous boats, both large and small, dotted Las Palmas' harbour, behind which rose a series of flat topped hills, becoming higher towards the interior, until their summits were draped in clouds. Situated on the slopes of a hill overlooking the harbour, the low, white cottages, interspersed with palm trees and lush foliage and a church spire towering above the buildings, formed a striking picture. Added to this was a wide, golden beach and deep blue sea.

As the ship dropped anchor the sea was immediately dotted with numerous small boats containing vendors eager to sell bananas and oranges, as well as souvenirs. These vendors scrambled up rope ladders on the side of the ship, carrying their baskets of wares for sale, which they proceeded to spread out on the deck. There were beautifully embroidered cloths, filigree brooches, felt hats, dolls, fruit and flowers.

This was a welcome diversion for the passengers, who wasted no time in buying their goods, amidst some haggling over the prices, while other passengers watched with interest the local divers who spent their time diving for money thrown over the side of the ship into the sea.

After a six hours' visit for restocking the ship with coal, fresh vegetables, meat and fruit, the Tintagel Castle weighed anchor and steamed away as the passengers stood on deck, watching the lights of the town begin to twinkle in the dusk until the island disappeared from view.

The sea was calmer now as they continued on their journey along the coast of Africa, passing three days later within sight of Cape Verde in French Senegal, the most westerly point of Africa. The sunny days were a delight to Daisy and her companions, who spent as much time as possible up on deck in the fresh air.

The Cadets soon discovered that there was very little entertainment arranged for the passengers, and the Captain willingly allowed them to hold services in the sitting room in the evenings.

The ship was on its eighth day of the voyage when the passengers suddenly caught sight of a large shoal of fish, leaping gracefully out of the water and disappearing again under the waves. As no land was in sight, anything unusual was a welcome diversion from looking at the endless sea, which gave one the feeling of being completely isolated from civilization.

As the ship neared the equator on the eleventh day of the voyage, the temperature rose and the young women, dressed in their long navy blue dresses with high collars, felt the heat intensely. Daisy, mopping her brow, turned to Jessie.

"I wonder how we'll cope with the heat once we reach South Africa," she remarked.

No voyage would be complete without a "Crossing the Line" ceremony, with King Neptune seated on his throne, busily lathering some of the sailors and male passengers with flour and water, and shaving them with a two foot long wooden razor. The crew had rigged up a special canvas salt-water bath, where those taking part were unceremoniously dumped, much to the amusement of the onlookers. A special afternoon tea followed, enabling the passengers to mingle with each other and make new friends.

One of the miners approached Daisy and engaged her in a conversation.

"I doubt whether all these young ladies will remain single for long once you arrive in South Africa," he grinned, "because there are plenty of miners looking for wives."

"Well," Daisy retorted, "I for one haven't come to look for a husband. If I had wanted one I would have found one in England. I've come to do a job of work in South Africa, and I mean to do it!"

As Christmas Day approached the crew busied themselves decorating the dining room, while the Cadets sang Christmas carols and several of the passengers joined in. How strange it felt to be so far from home at Christmas time. For Daisy, and probably for many of the other Cadets, this would be their first Christmas away from their families.

Christmas Day dawned bright and sunny, the sea was pleasantly calm and the passengers were in good spirits. The cooks prepared a sumptuous dinner for the passengers, which they greatly enjoyed, and the passengers joined the Cadets in singing Christmas carols.

"And so ends our first hot Christmas," Jessie laughed, as the friends prepared for bed that night. Daisy was busily writing a letter to Amelia, telling her about the sea voyage and all that they had seen.

"It won't be the last, either," Daisy replied, reflecting on the life that lay ahead of them, "and we'll be landing in South Africa in the middle of the summer."

On Boxing Day everyone turned their attention to packing their belongings, in preparation for the ship's arrival in Cape Town on December 27th. Excitement was running high now, with the realization that their new life in a new country was about to begin.

CHAPTER 8

A NEW LAND AND A NEW CHALLENGE

Early in the morning of December 27th 1896, the *Tintagel Castle* steamed into Cape Town harbour, giving the Cadets their first glimpse of the country to which they had come to preach the Gospel. Crowding the decks, the excited passengers viewed the picturesque scene before them.

Table Mountain, with its fluffy white "table cloth" of clouds draped carelessly over its flat summit, loomed magnificently over the city spread around its base. To the south, smaller mountains varying in size extended to Cape Point, the furthermost point of the Cape of Good Hope. North of Cape Town the land was fairly flat near the edge of the sea, with a high mountain range extending further along the coast and inland. In the city itself, several impressive buildings could be seen.

"Cape Town is so beautiful!" Daisy exclaimed, hardly able to contain her excitement, "I can scarcely believe we are actually here." This was the moment of which she had dreamed for so long, and now her dreams were about to become a reality. She too, would be a missionary in South Africa, and bring God's word to both black and white people, just as her friend's father had done so many years before.

Standing on deck, Daisy was thankful for the slight breeze that flapped the hem of her heavy, uncomfortably warm, navy blue uniform about her ankles. Her wide blue eyes, dimpled cheeks and light brown hair shaded by the large blue bonnet she wore, gave her slightly built frame the appearance of a young woman even younger than her eighteen years.

"How different this is from England," Daisy remarked to Jessie, "where everyone is now celebrating the Christmas season in cold weather. I wonder what this country will hold for us."

"Plenty of surprises, no doubt," responded Jessie, leaning over the railing watching the dark-skinned stevedores on the quayside and the people waiting to welcome the passengers, while little boys fished placidly from the dock.

A hearty welcome awaited the Cadets from the group of Salvation Army Officers assembled on the dock. All at once the brass band accompanying them struck up a cheerful tune, making the young women feel instantly at home. Chatting and hurrying down the gangway, the nineteen Cadets and their Officer were soon on the dock, where Colonel Rauch and Major Swain welcomed them to their new land.

After the speeches the Cadets, sweltering in the unaccustomed heat and clutching their Gladstone bags, lined up behind the band and marched to the Salvation Army's Territorial Headquarters in Loop Street.

Daisy glanced around her with interest. Palm trees lined the streets, giving an occasional patch of shade, and to her surprise she noticed that many of the buildings were modern and solidly built.

I wonder if we'll see any wild animals, she thought, but to her relief they saw none.

Perhaps my ideas were a little out of date, she mused, recalling her preconceived ideas of South Africa being a land of thick jungle with wild animals prowling around the homesteads.

At last the Cadets arrived thankfully at the hall, where refreshments awaited them. The Commissioner welcomed them, told them what their duties were to be, and where they would be sent. This being their first appointment, they were given the title of Lieutenant, and were divided into two groups. One group would stay at the Headquarters in Cape Town, and the other would be sent to the village of Wynberg nearby.

Also present at the gathering was Staff Captain Mrs. Stevens, who welcomed Daisy to South Africa.

"I'm so happy to see you, Daisy," she exclaimed, "because as you know, your mother has asked me to be your mother in this land. You will always be welcome to visit our family here in Cape Town, and it will be my pleasure to help you in any way I am able."

Daisy held her hands warmly, feeling the tears well up in her eyes. How typical of her mother to think of her every need. She was already missing her mother, and no doubt would miss her even more as time went by.

"Thank you, Mrs. Stevens. You are so kind—and I am also looking forward to meeting your daughter Ethel," she replied.

Daisy found herself among the group chosen to go to Wynberg, which, a few days later, were escorted to the railway station and helped to board the train. From a seat beside the window, she had a good view of Cape Town's well-established suburbs with their neat houses flashing by, and pine trees on the mountainside.

That evening the young women were housed in a large room that had been converted from a barn, with its floor smoothed and hardened with layers of mud. It was furnished with beds, a few washstands, water jugs and bowls.

"What an exciting few days it has been," Daisy smiled. "We've arrived in a new country, had a short stay in Cape Town, and here we are preparing to sleep in an old barn!"

Some time during the night Daisy was awakened by a peculiar, grunting sound.

"Did you hear that noise?" she whispered loudly, hoping someone else had been awakened. Stories of wild animals at once sprang to mind, and she lay there uneasily for a few moments. At last, gathering up her courage, she fumbled in the dark for her candle and matches on the table beside her bed.

In the flickering candlelight the mystery was solved. There, half drowned and floundering in a bowl of water on the washstand, was a huge rat!

During the next week the young women spent their time walking around Wynberg, becoming acquainted with the small village and selling copies of *"The War Cry."* Always in twos, they set out on their rounds, delighting in their walks through the cool pine forests carpeted with wild flowers, and stopping to admire the plumbago hedges, with their blue-grey flowers, growing in front of many of the neatly kept houses.

On January 13th, Daisy was summoned to her Commanding Officer who informed her that she would be given the task of running a school for children who were the offspring of mixed parentage (black and white, and were known as Coloureds) in Robertson, a small town in the Cape Province. She would work in conjunction with Captain van Beek, who had already gone on ahead to begin missionary work. As she had always wanted to teach, she was delighted that she had been given this task and looked forward to the challenge.

Leaving Wynberg for Robertson at the end of January, Daisy found the scenery fascinating. Winding round the mountains on its hundred mile journey, the train passed lush vineyards in picturesque valleys, clusters of bright yellow mimosa bushes and patches of gleaming white arum lilies nestling alongside streams.

Suddenly, to her astonishment, a magnificent ostrich appeared from behind a clump of bushes and ran at an amazing speed alongside the train. The real Africa, thought Daisy.

Dotting the hillsides were the round domed huts of the black Africans, whose little children, often playing completely naked, ran laughing towards the train with their little hands outstretched, hoping someone would throw them some pennies.

Daisy looked out of the window with interest as the train came to a halt at the little station in Robertson. She could see Captain van Beek, her face creased with smiles, standing on the platform waiting to meet her. Accompanying her was an African man with his horse drawn two-wheeled Cape cart, who wasted no time in loading Daisy's belongings into it. Soon they were headed along the dusty road leading into the little town.

Robertson, its wide, tree-lined streets boasting only two or three shops, was quaint and beautiful, tucked in among the mountains. A small stream, pulsing from its source in the mountain, meandered down its slopes to spill itself lazily into a large dam in the valley, providing the town with its water supply.

Near the dam stood the newly constructed corrugated iron Salvation Army Hall, where the owner of the Cape cart off-loaded Daisy's luggage and bade them farewell.

Daisy explored her new home. Attached to the Hall was a bedroom, sitting room and kitchen. The kitchen furniture consisted of a packing case for storing groceries, an upturned box on which stood two buckets for fetching water from the dam, and an old table. There was no stove, thus cooking had to be done in the fireplace over two built-in bars. The bedroom and sitting room were equally sparsely furnished, with the inevitable mud floors and ceilings made of calico material, a plain, unbleached cotton cloth, stretched from wall to wall.

"I know it looks rather bleak," apologised Captain van Beek, "but I'm sure we will be able to make it more comfortable."

Undaunted, they set to work, using whatever material they could find, and with a little effort and ingenuity the cheerless rooms took on a cosier atmosphere.

From the bedroom window Daisy could see the Location, the township in which the Coloured families lived in row upon row of neatly kept houses divided by quince hedges.

"We will be starting up a school in the hall," Captain van Beek informed Daisy, "so we will have an interesting time ahead of us. It will be your task to run the school, while I carry on with the mission work."

"I'm ready, Captain," Daisy replied, her eyes sparkling with anticipation.

Word soon spread that the "girl in a blue bonnet" was to open a school for their children at the end of January. The mothers grasped this opportunity, as there was a shortage of schools in that area, and enrolment began at a brisk pace on the first day of the school year.

Daisy asked each child to bring a slate, as no exercise books were as yet available, and some food for their lunch. She soon encountered her first obstacle. The children spoke High Dutch, a language that she did not understand. Thankfully this was overcome with the help of fourteen-year-old September, a Standard 4 pupil (Grade 6) who could speak English and High Dutch. He acted as interpreter, so it was not long before Daisy and the children were able to communicate.

Daisy noticed that although the children were poorly dressed, they were spotlessly clean, a fact which pleased her. She was also impressed by their generosity. On many occasions she was shyly offered a cold sweet potato that some child had brought for lunch.

She discovered their natural love and talent for music. Singing effortlessly in tune, their small bodies swaying rhythmically in time to the music, their dark faces beamed with enjoyment.

This is the way to their hearts, thought Daisy, and it is through music that I will teach them.

During the next few months as the children progressed and Daisy was learning to communicate more easily with them, she taught them to sing some of the cheerful Salvation Army songs. Captain van Beek arranged to have some musical instruments sent to the school and soon the children had their own little band consisting of tambourines, a drum and a violin. Eventually they could perform their musical drills with precision.

Daisy made an effort to meet the parents of the children in the Corps, and became friends with them. When their children performed during the services, they beamed in appreciation. The young "girl in a blue bonnet" had taught their children well!

As the months went by, Daisy taught the children scarf drills to learn precision, and dumb bell drills, where short bars with a weight on each end were used to strengthen their muscles.

Captain van Beek decided that it was time for Daisy to hold a demonstration. Enlisting the help of some of the mothers, they made a costume for each child with material donated by the local store. The girls wore red blouses and blue skirts and the boys wore red shirts and blue trousers.

As the No. 1 Corps of the Salvation Army in the neighbouring town of Montagu had offered their barracks for a night, Daisy and her party of excited children set off early one February morning in a four-horse tent wagon, driven by the father of one of the pupils.

The mountains were ablaze with brilliant wild flowers following recent rains, and Daisy was filled with gratitude to God for all the beauty around her on that lovely summer morning.

She had grown to love her little pupils, and was learning to converse with them in Dutch. Not only was she interested in giving these children an education, but she considered their spiritual growth of prime importance. Captain van Beek was an inspiring role model to her, and she was grateful for her comforting hugs when she felt homesick for Amelia and her family.

That evening, after a rousing reception from the Montagu Corps, the "Robertson Red Jackets," as they were called, delighted their audience with their dumb-bell drills and action songs. Beaming with pleasure at the sound of applause, the children realised that they had achieved something worthwhile.

Next morning at sunrise, Daisy and the children set out for the neighbouring town of Swellendam, a ten hours journey by wagon. None of the children had been so far away from home before, and to them it was an exciting adventure.

"Look, there's an ostrich farm!" shouted one of the boys, pointing to a large enclosure in which a number of ostriches strode about on their powerful legs.

The road wound around the slopes of the flower covered mountains until at last they arrived at an orange farm, where the horses were brought to a halt for a welcome rest. Acres of trees laden with ripe golden fruit appeared before them, and the children gazed longingly at the oranges. Daisy, however, asked the farmer only for a drink of water for each child and for the horses, but the kindly old Boer farmer, with typical hospitality, loaded them with fruit, much to their delight.

The No. 1 Corps in Swellendam gave them a warm welcome and the children, smartly dressed in their new costumes, sang tunefully and performed their drills effortlessly. They charged sixpence admission and the hall was full. Daisy had scored another triumph with her willing pupils.

Homeward bound the following day, the skies suddenly clouded over. All at once the wind sprang up and the covered wagon was pelted with rain; but Daisy, having had the foresight to bring a few blankets, tucked the children up and hoped for the best.

It was a tired, bedraggled group that was met by the Captain that evening, but the children's faces were shining with the memory of a wonderful outing, and each child was eager to tell her of their adventures.

When Commissioner Ridsel and Brigadier Howe came to Robertson a fortnight later they asked to see the children in action, having heard of their success at No. 1 Corps. Duly impressed, they suggested that twelve of the children should take part in the great Congress to be held in Cape Town early in the new year.

"We've no time to lose, Daisy," Captain van Beek remarked, "so we'll have to ask some of the mothers to help us make a costume for each child."

Their outfits consisted of yellow shirts trimmed with red, navy blue skirts or pants, white shoes and bells on their wrists and ankles. The children were excited at the prospect of travelling in a train to Cape Town, as many of them had never been in a train before, and had never even seen the sea.

Christmas passed in a flurry of activity, with well-attended services in the Salvation Army Hall.

"This is my second Christmas away from home," declared Daisy pensively, thinking of Amelia, Polly and Nellie celebrating together in Ealing. No doubt James, his wife Florence and their three sons, Stanley, Bernard and Leonard, would have joined them. How she longed to see her family again.

"How quickly the time has passed. We arrived in South Africa a whole year ago!" she exclaimed, as she settled down at the kitchen table after dinner, to write her mother a long letter.

"Yes," replied Captain van Beek, "and just think about what you have achieved in that time!"

At last it was time for Daisy and the children to set off for Cape Town. After a cheerful good-bye to parents, they boarded the train at seven o'clock in the evening, arriving at seven o'clock in the morning of New Year's Eve, a time of great merry-making in Cape Town.

Coming from a quiet country town into the noise and bustle of the city over-awed some of the children, and it was some time before they were at last settled in their billets, where they soon made themselves at home.

On the Field Day they took part in the Junior Demonstration, as well as in the Grand Carnival that night. With their eyes fixed on Daisy, they went through their drills faultlessly, oblivious of the great crowd of people watching them. On the last day of the Congress they again performed at the Citadel, going through all their drills and also playing some tunes with their comb bands (where they blew onto their combs) accompanied by little Jacob January, one of the students, on the autoharp.

Envoy Eayrs, who was present at the meeting, was impressed with their performance.

"If you come to my shop tomorrow, I'll fit you all out with a pair of new shoes," he promised, and the following morning the excited children visited his shop to receive the much-appreciated gift. Next day they departed reluctantly from the sea and all the other attractions of Cape Town, arriving that evening in Robertson.

The Commissioner had been impressed with Daisy's efforts. During the short space of a year she had built up a school from nothing and established it firmly, and her ability to communicate with children was becoming obvious. He felt the time was ripe for her to move on to gain more experience and recalled her to Cape Town.

Daisy parted with sadness from the lovely little village and from Captain van Beek, who had helped her so much and had comforted her in her bouts of homesickness. But partings were to become a familiar part of her career, for a Salvation Army Officer was seldom stationed for long in one area.

As the train departed slowly from the railway station, Daisy, leaning out of the carriage window, waved to the children and Captain van Beek who were standing on the platform. The children began to sing spontaneously, their voices slowly fading in the distance as the train puffed on its way to Cape Town.

Sinking onto the carriage seat, Daisy wiped the tears from her eyes. She would miss the smiling faces of her pupils and the kindly guidance of Captain van Beek.

In a letter to the Salvation Army Headquarters in London, Daisy wrote:

> *I must say that these children love to come to the meetings and hear about Jesus and His love, and they can answer questions on Bible subjects in a way that does them credit. Many of them are trying hard to live good lives and to live for Jesus. One boy, fourteen years old, named Jacob Cornelius, volunteered to the*

> *penitent form one night and got thoroughly saved, and it does one's heart good to hear him testify and pray. He is an example to all the other children in the school, and does all he can to get his companions saved.*
>
> · *He was so anxious to convert his friend that he said to him: "Harry, if you will only get saved, I'll give you my pet canary!" We believe he will make a good Officer one day. These juniors are very enthusiastic and willingly sell The War Cry, and their parents are delighted when they see their names on the Roll of Honour.*
>
> *During my stay in Robertson I learned to love these dear little dark-skinned children very much, and when the time came for me to say farewell, they came, bringing their little gifts. One lad said to his mother: "Please kill a chicken, Mother, and cook it for Lieutenant to eat on her journey." Another had nothing else to give, so she brought a lock of the baby's hair.*

How quickly the year had passed by, Daisy reflected, and what an interesting and rewarding year it had been. She had learned so much and made so many new friends. Now it was time for her to move on, this time to the beautiful city of Cape Town. She felt as though she was closing a chapter in the book of her life, and turning the page to a new one. What new experiences awaited her, and what new friendships would she form, she wondered as the train approached her destination.

CHAPTER 9

GETTING TO KNOW CAPE TOWN

Daisy was relieved to note that a Salvation Army Officer was standing on the platform, ready to meet her, when the train came to a stop at Cape Town's railway station.

The porter wasted no time in loading her luggage onto his cart, and accompanied by the Officer, she was soon seated in a horse-drawn carriage, headed for the Salvation Army Headquarters.

Settling down comfortably on the leather seat, she surveyed the passing scene with interest. Peering upwards out of the window, she could see the pine covered slopes of towering Table Mountain, its summit draped with fluffy white clouds commonly known as 'the tablecloth.' White-washed houses with elaborate teak doors and quaint fanlights, green shuttered windows and inviting verandahs, nestled between solidly built buildings.

"Cape Town is as beautiful as ever," she remarked happily, noting the restful gardens, street vendors and buskers. Flower sellers displayed their colourful flowers stacked near the road, people walked in the shade of the old oak trees and others rode by on horseback or in carriages.

The Salvation Army Commissioner gave Daisy a warm welcome at the Headquarters, where she was to be briefed on her new assignment.

"I am pleased with the work you have done in Robertson, Lieutenant Quarterman, and I feel it is time for you to gain further experience," the

Commissioner said. "As you have already gained valuable experience working in the slums of London,' he continued, "you should be able to cope with the task I am about to give you."

Daisy listened intently, wondering where she would be sent next.

"I am promoting you to the rank of Captain, and you will be assisted by Lieutenant Farley. You will be working among the Coloured people who live and work near Cape Town's docks."

Grateful for the opportunity of working in the city she had grown to love, Daisy smiled happily as she thanked the Commissioner.

Daisy spent the night at the home of Staff Captain Mrs. Stevens, where the family welcomed her warmly.

"We're so happy you've been transferred to Cape Town, Daisy," her hostess remarked, "now we will be able to see you more often. As you know, our home will always be your 'home away from home' in this country."

Daisy was heartened by the warm welcome of her mother's friend, and resolved to write a long letter to her mother as soon as she was settled in her new post.

Daisy and Lieutenant Farley were taken to their new home and workplace, a humble room attached to the Salvation Army hall, little more than a shack, near the tough dockside area. Setting to work, the two young women unpacked their belongings and cleaned the hall in preparation for holding their meetings.

On Sunday morning they stood at the door of the hall, smiling and ready to welcome the local people. The women arrived, spotlessly clean with a fresh apron over their skirts, their heads covered with a colourful four cornered scarf tied at the nape of their neck. The men came, dressed in their ordinary working clothes, for after the service they would have to go to their boats and prepare them for the following day's fishing.

These kindly folk sang the cheerful Salvation Army songs with enthusiasm, clapping in time to the music, their bodies swaying rhythmically.

Being so close to the docks, the hall was inhabited by rats, a fact that didn't seem to bother the congregation, but which filled the young women with apprehension.

"Keep your eyes open while I pray, please Captain," begged Lieutenant Farley, who had a horror of a rat suddenly landing on their laps.

Daisy and Lieutenant Farley always went out together, for in this tough neighbourhood it was unwise to walk alone. However, even the toughest men left them in peace to sell their copies of *The War Cry*.

Walking down the narrow streets, where the houses were joined together in long rows, they looked around them with interest. Snoek, a type of fish, was freshly gutted and hung out on lines in their back yards, drying in the sun. These people, whose staple diet was fish, earned their living from the sea.

Daisy stepped aside as a fisherman with a long wooden cart, laden with snoek, passed by, leaving behind a strong smell of fish.

During the week, house visiting was one of their duties they enjoyed, and they were soon making friends with the local inhabitants. At night though, they took no chances, and were constantly on guard against intruders by barricading themselves in their room with chairs propped up against the door.

Once a week Daisy and Lieutenant Farley visited various ships docked in the harbour, to sell *The War Cry* and to hold services on board. The rough manners of the seamen left them undeterred. They had a job to do—to preach the Gospel to all—and they were determined to do it.

There was much to see at the docks. On the beach at the foreshore, numerous open boats, their bows turned seawards, were ready to launch, the fishermen bustling about with their oars, anchor ropes and tackle boxes. When the fleet put to sea, bobbing over the waves, the sight was unforgettable.

When the boats returned laden with fish, the beach was crowded with brightly dressed Malay women, (descendants of settlers from

Malaysia), Malay priests, fish carts waiting for the catch and small boys wearing fezzes on their heads. A flurry of activity ensued, the fish carts piled high with the day's catch and the loud 'paah, paah, paah of the fish horns ringing joyously out over the city to inform the residents that they had fish for sale. But there was no rest for the weary fishermen; boats had to be scrubbed clean and canvas covers placed over sails and spars. Only then could they depart for a well earned rest, leaving behind the remains of the gutted fish for the greedy, squawking gulls.

During this period of work at the docks, Daisy had an almost constant cough, aggravated by nearly three months of rainy weather. Eventually she was persuaded to see a doctor.

"I advise you to leave Cape Town as soon as possible," he said, "and move to a drier climate. "As you know, you have a spot on one lung and you need to live at a higher altitude where the air is dry and warm."

When Daisy reported the doctor's diagnosis to the Commissioner, he was most concerned about her health, and a week later he sent for her again.

"It is time for another change, Captain Quarterman," he told her, "I've arranged for you to be sent to Queenstown where the climate should suit you better. It is a small inland town in the Cape Province, inhabited by numerous descendants of the 1820 Settlers from Britain. Lieutenant Ethel Stevens will accompany you, and Ensign Walter Scott will escort you on your journey."

Daisy heard this news with mixed feelings. She was enjoying the challenge of building up a congregation in the dock area, and now she would be moved to another town.

In a letter to her mother, mentioning her transfer, Daisy wrote:

> *At least I'll have Ethel with me, and it will be nice to*
> *work with someone I know so well. You will be pleased*
> *to know, Mother, that Mrs. Stevens has been very kind*
> *to me and has treated me as her own daughter.*

Another Officer was assigned to replace Daisy, thus opening up the way for her departure. Packing her luggage for the journey, she placed the photograph of her family in her trunk and prepared for bed.

Tomorrow will bring its own surprises, she reflected, snuggling down under the blankets, and was soon fast asleep.

CHAPTER 10

DAISY MEETS ENSIGN WALTER SCOTT

Daisy was up early the next morning, completing her last minute packing in preparation for her train journey to Queenstown.

Hurrying to answer the knock at the door, she found Ensign Walter Scott standing on the doorstep. For a moment her gaze took in the appearance of the slightly built young man of medium height with thick, dark brown hair and bright blue eyes. Above his strong mouth was a well-clipped moustache.

After introducing himself he carried her luggage to the carriage, where Ethel was already seated and excited at the prospect of spending time with Daisy.

Daisy gave Lieutenant Farley a farewell hug, Ensign Scott helped her into the carriage and the horses plodded off along the street, bound for Cape Town's railway station.

Giving a final farewell wave out of the carriage window, Daisy felt a surge of excitement. She would soon be seeing another part of this beautiful, interesting country. Her dream of seeing far-away places was at last coming true.

The train, winding slowly through the mountains, opened up vistas of high mountain peaks, steep ravines and streams sparkling in the sunlight as they rushed down into the valleys on their way to the sea.

Daisy, accustomed to England's gentle, rolling green hills, found the scenery in the Cape Province awe-inspiring and fascinating; so much so, in fact, that she was scarcely aware of her companions. Eventually her gaze drifted toward Walter, who was recounting his family history.

"My grandfather, Alexander Forbes, at the age of twenty-seven, came from Longford in Ireland, on a ship called the *East Indian*, which sailed from Cork on the twelfth of February 1820. With him was his brother Edward, who had with him his wife Harriet and their two children. They were part of William Parker's party of 1820 Settlers. Later he married Jane Thomas who was also from a Settler family from Ireland. The marriage took place in St. George's Anglican Cathedral in Grahamstown, in September 1826, and they settled on their eight hundred acre farm Waaiplaats, where they kept twenty head of cattle. Farming was a new occupation for him, as he was a shoemaker by trade.

"The settlers were harassed from time to time by the Xhosa tribe who lived on the other side of the river. They attacked the farmers, took their possessions and set fire to the bush surrounding their homes, bringing death and destruction to a peaceful, prosperous land.

"One morning my grandmother, along with her six children, was washing clothing in the spring in the river when suddenly they were surrounded by a group of Xhosa men, who began to harass them.

My grandfather left the house and went down to find out what they wanted. They seized him, and despite his pleas and the pleas of his wife and children, they stabbed him to death with their spears.

"Picking up her youngest child, eighteen month old Henry, my grandmother ran for her life, followed by her other four children, to the safety of their neighbour, Mr. Staples. Later they discovered that the Forbes family home had been burned to the ground, as well as all their clothes, food and possessions."

"How sad," commented Daisy, her imagination conjuring up the scene of destruction.

"And it was Christmas Eve as well," added Walter, "so my grandfather was buried on their farm on the 26th December, 1834. He was about forty-one years old.

"However, many other families had similar tales to tell. The Richardson family was forced to flee as well, just before Christmas. Mrs. Richardson had just placed a very large plum cake in the oven, which she left in her haste to leave the farm. Two months later two of their sons were patrolling with a party. As they approached the house they thought of the plum cake that had been left in the oven. To their great surprise they discovered that the cake was still good!"

"I can just imagine how they tucked into that plum cake," laughed Daisy.

"But that wasn't the end of the story," continued Walter, "because six months after my grandfather's death their son Alexander was born, so my grandmother had six children to bring up without the help of a husband.

"One of my grandparents' six children was my mother, Anne Forbes. She married my father, James Scott, who had emigrated from Edinburgh. After their marriage they settled in Fort Beaufort where my father ran a thriving general dealer's store.

"About 1878 the British Military Garrison was withdrawn from Fort Beaufort, and the Xhosas once again harassed the settlers, causing much suffering and loss. Businesses closed down and many families moved elsewhere. When the Xhosas burned down my father's business, he moved with his family to Queenstown, where he opened up another trading store. He died in 1890."

Ethel opened the picnic basket her mother had prepared for them, and the three tired travellers were thankful for the delicious food. How kind everyone had been, Daisy reflected, tucking into a juicy piece of chicken.

"I hope you are going to like Queenstown, Captain," Walter was saying as his blue eyes surveyed the slightly built young woman, noting her dimples when she smiled. "It's my hometown, so I'm pleased to be going back there for a short while."

"I'm sure we'll be very happy there," Daisy replied. "I've been told it's a pretty town."

The train journey seemed never ending, with the train stopping at every little siding and railway station; and as the sun began to sink behind the hills they were thankful for the warm rugs they had brought with them.

Settling down to sleep, Daisy thought with affection of her mother's practical nature. The rug she had given her had been used often, while the soft, chamois chest protector kept her warm on the coldest days. Although she had often been tempted to use some of the half-crowns so lovingly sewn between its folds, she had resisted the temptation, keeping them instead for a 'really rainy day.'

After several delays, caused by engine trouble during the journey, the train came to a halt at Queenstown station at four o'clock in the morning, and the three companions, upon alighting from the train, were met by a blast of icy wind.

"It's been snowing!" gasped Daisy, "I didn't know it snowed in this part of the country!"

"It very seldom snows," replied Walter, trudging across the thick snow as he carried the trunks and suitcases to the waiting room.

"The door's locked!" exclaimed Walter in frustration, while Daisy and Ethel stood shivering against the wall. Walter looked around hopefully for his brother, but there was no sign of him. Most probably a snowdrift had held up his horse and carriage. They had no choice but to pace up and down on the platform in an effort to keep warm.

So much for sending me to a warm, dry climate, thought Daisy wryly.

Eventually Walter's brother arrived, and the three cold and weary travellers slid thankfully into the carriage.

The Scott family made Daisy and Ethel feel at home with their warm hospitality, and after spending a day and night there, they helped them move into their new home, a small but comfortable house with a wood burning stove in the kitchen.

Ethel had noticed Walter's attentiveness to Daisy.

"He seems very interested in you," she remarked. "He has hardly taken his eyes off you since he met you."

Daisy's cheeks coloured with embarrassment.

"I'm not interested in him, or in any other man!" she retorted, "I have a job of work to do."

Ethel smiled but said nothing more. A comfortable comradeship existed between them as their families were close friends.

The two young women soon found that the people of Queenstown were rather reserved. Progress in their work was difficult and donations trickled in very slowly.

"I'm sure these people think we don't need to eat," commented Ethel, after a discouraging day selling *The War Cry*. "I don't think we've sold more than a dozen copies today, and we've walked from one end of the town to the other."

"Never mind. At least the baker has invited us to his home for dinner tomorrow night," Daisy reminded her.

Ethel's face lit up. "Well, if his cooking is as good as his baking, we'll be treated to a good square meal," she smiled.

The kindly baker proved to be a good friend, who not only supplied them with a loaf of freshly baked bread each day, but arrived one morning with some meat and vegetables. Concerned for their welfare, he insisted on them coming to dinner at his home at least once a week, when he piled their plates high with delicious food.

His wife, a lonely invalid confined to a wheelchair, looked forward to their visits. Every morning, before going on their rounds, they called in to see to her needs.

Gradually the people of Queenstown began to accept them into the community and their work progressed. They also began to feel at home there, because many of the inhabitants had immigrated from

England, Scotland, Wales and Ireland, and enjoyed talking about "the old country."

However, after six months in Queenstown, Daisy's cough was no better, and the doctor advised her to move further inland, where the air was warm and drier.

On receiving the doctor's report, the Commissioner decided to send her to Beaconsfield in Kimberley, a diamond mining town in Griqualand West.

Daisy received this news with mixed feelings, for during their stay in Queenstown Walter had been a frequent visitor, even though he was stationed in Cape Town, and she had become fond of him, despite herself. Now his visits would come to an end and she would miss him.

A few days before Daisy and Ethel departed for Kimberley, Ethel brought in the post.

"There's a letter for you, Daisy," smiled Ethel, handing her a letter with a familiar handwriting. It was from Walter.

Daisy took the letter and went outside to the bench in the shade of a tree, where she opened up the neatly written letter, her hand trembling a little as she read it.

> *I have loved you from the moment I first met you, Daisy, and you would make me very happy if you would consent to becoming my wife.*

Daisy sat there for a long time, turning over in her mind the proposal Walter had sent her. She knew she would be very happy being married to Walter, and yet she hesitated. Was this the right time to make such an important decision? After all, she was only twenty-one years old.

With a sigh she came inside and sat down at the table to write a reply.

> *Dear Walter, I am honoured that you care enough*
> *for me to ask me to be your wife, and as you know, I*
> *care a great deal for you as well. However, I feel that*
> *I am still too young for marriage and I have not yet*
> *accomplished all that I have set out to do. I do hope*
> *you will understand.*

With a heavy heart she placed the letter in the postbox and returned to the house to resume her packing for the trip she and Ethel would be making to Kimberley.

CHAPTER 11

THE FIRST SIGNS OF WAR

A few days later, when the train steamed into the railway station at Kimberley, Daisy and Ethel were eager to see the town. After all, Kimberley had become world famous.

Early prospectors, searching for diamonds on a farm called Vooruitzicht in the northern Cape, sent their drunken servant to a nearby hill with the instruction that he was to stay there until he found a diamond. Intending this as a punishment for his behaviour, they were astounded when he returned, sober, a few days later, clutching a few shiny stones.

Fleetwood Rawstone and his fellow diggers rushed to stake their claim on the hill, which they named "Colesberg Kopse" on July 16th, 1871. News travelled fast, and soon hopeful diggers arrived from all over the country and from many other parts of the world as well.

The site was called De Beers New Rush, after the De Beer brothers who owned the farm, and in 1873 the town was named Kimberley after the British Colonial Secretary, Lord Kimberley.

Colesberg Kopse disintegrated as scores of miners dug deep into the ground around the diamond bearing kimberlite pipe. The hole became bigger and more chaotic, with cables and pulleys strung from one side to the other, while the miners worked long hours with one purpose in mind: to become rich!

Conditions in the camp were unsanitary and dangerous, with miners living in tents and under pieces of wood or corrugated iron.

Eventually Cecil John Rhodes and Barney Barnarto acquired an interest in the Kimberley Mine, leading to the creation of De Beers Consolidated Mines Limited, a powerful organization which became world famous.

By 1898, however, the town had progressed. The tarpaulins, corrugated iron sheets and unruly diggers were gone, and in their place were substantially built homes, hotels and municipal buildings. Horses and carts and carriages carried goods and people on the dusty roads under a clear, sunny sky.

Daisy and Ethel were soon settled in a small brick house with a corrugated iron roof, and after unpacking they walked to the "Big Hole" to see for themselves the huge cavern left behind by the early diggers.

About a week later a letter arrived, addressed to Daisy. It was from Walter, to let her know that he would wait until she felt the time was right to marry him. Thus began a series of letters between them during the nine months that Daisy and Ethel were stationed in Kimberley.

The dry air in that semi-desert part of the country was so beneficial to Daisy that the patch on her lung healed and her cough disappeared.

During that time they had made friends with the local people, whom they found to be so friendly and helpful that they felt reluctant to leave after receiving notice of yet another transfer, this time to the town of Mafeking. Situated near the border of Bechuanaland (Botswana) and on the main railway route to Rhodesia (Zimbabwe), it was an important railway junction, and the railway line, built by the British, was vital for the transportation of goods. Relations between the British and the Boers were becoming strained, with the possibility of the outbreak of war, and the British were mindful that the railway line would have to be protected.

The nineteenth century in South Africa had been a time of war and conflict. Boer, Briton, Zulu, Xhosa and various African tribes were all fighting for land, and the Boers had proved themselves fierce and formidable fighters.

In fact, there had been periodic unrest in South Africa ever since the Dutch East India Company sent Jan van Riebeeck to the Cape in 1652. He established a settlement to provide meat and fresh vegetables to its fleets journeying to and from the Spice Islands of the East Indies and also built a fort for protection, as well as a hospital for sick sailors.

At that time, the only inhabitants of the Cape were the Hottentot tribes, who kept cattle, which they moved from place to place in search of grazing.

Then, in 1688, a group of French Huguenots arrived at the Cape Colony, adding to the white population. Cape Town grew and flourished and some of the settlers moved further inland, away from the fierce winds, to establish farms and vineyards.

In 1795, a British expeditionary force took over the Cape at the request of the Prince of Orange, who was exiled in England when Holland became the Batavian Republic under French revolutionary tutelage. The British flag replaced the Dutch flag for eight years, after which the Batavian Republic brought Dutch rule back to the Cape from 1803 to 1806. When the war against Napoleon resumed, the Batavian rulers at the Cape had no choice but to await the inevitable return of the British, who temporarily occupied the Cape in January 1806, pending the outcome of the war against Napoleon.

After the Battle of Waterloo and the defeat of Napoleon, the Netherlands, then a kingdom under the House of Orange, was generously treated by the European settlement of 1814, but the Cape of Good Hope went to Great Britain by concession. To boost the English speaking population at the Cape, about 5,000 immigrants arrived from England, Ireland, Scotland and Wales, and were settled near the eastern frontier of the colony. They became known as the 1820 Settlers and were to have a profound effect on the development of the country.

The Dutch settlers in the Cape colony, called the Boers, resented British rule. Many of them began to move inland, and in 1835 the

Great Trek began in earnest, with these Boers, called the Voortrekkers, loading their covered wagons pulled by oxen. They left the Cape and trekked inland, facing many dangers and formidable mountain ranges, and found fertile valleys where they established farms.

Over the years the British and the Boers clashed on various issues, then, because the British were ruling the Cape Colony and had annexed the Transvaal in 1877, the bitter Boers waged war against the British and defeated them in a bloody battle on Majuba Hill in 1881. This resulted in Britain recognizing the independence of the Transvaal, where the Boers were well entrenched.

However, when gold was discovered in the Witwatersrand area of the Transvaal in 1886, prospectors from all over the world, including many from Britain, descended on the newly formed town of Johannesburg in the hope of finding gold.

When these newcomers, now living on the Witwatersrand and outnumbering the Boer residents, demanded equal voting rights, President Kruger refused to extend the franchise. He then came under increasing pressure from the British High Commissioner, Sir Alfred Milner, to reform the Boer Republic. Sir Alfred regarded Kruger's refusal as an insult to the British. There was much resentment on both sides.

Britain, desiring to remain the historical centre of the world's banking and finance, needed gold. Its discovery in the Transvaal prompted Britain to extend its influence further than the Cape and Natal.

The Boers had been under British rule before and were still smarting from the annexation of the Transvaal by the British in 1877, as well as their clashes with the British during the First Boer War that took place from 1870 to 1871. Now they would have to capitulate again or fight to retain their independence.

President Paul Kruger, President of the South African Republic in the Transvaal and President Marthinus Steyn of the Orange Free State Republic, were determined to maintain the independence of their states.

Tensions began to build up over the next two years, with Milner insisting that if Kruger did not agree to reform, war would be inevitable. Kruger was in no mood to give in.

Rudyard Kipling informed his readers of the *London Times* that Kruger was "savage and uncontrolled," thus fanning patriotic fervour. Kruger's followers, however, regarded him as a wise, benevolent father figure.

It was under this cloud of uncertainty that the two young women found themselves once more preparing for a train journey to take up their posts in a strange town, amidst the rumblings of war.

It was not surprising, therefore, that Daisy's friends in Kimberley and Cape Town were dismayed when they heard the news that she and Ethel had been transferred to Mafeking. In letters to them they pointed out the danger of two young women going upcountry while there was so much trouble in the countryside.

Besides, they wrote, *people are leaving there daily, bound for the safety of Cape Town. The trains are full of women and children being evacuated. Anything could happen to you!*

I've been appointed to Mafeking for a good reason, Daisy replied firmly. *The women and children there need a helping hand while their men prepare for war. How can I refuse to go because of the danger when they have to face danger every day?*

The Commissioner had appointed Daisy, knowing of her fearlessness and strong sense of duty. He felt that the Salvationists in Mafeking should not be abandoned without any moral support at a time when anxiety was mounting due to the large Boer army rallying not very far from the town. Knowing what lay ahead of them, Daisy and Ethel prepared to depart from the safety of Kimberley to the uncertainty of life in Mafeking.

CHAPTER 12

DANGER IN MAFEKING

Leaving Kimberley the train set off on its 223 mile journey to Mafeking, near the borders of Bechuanaland and the Boer Republics. Situated 900 miles north of Cape Town, Kimberley had been laid out in 1885 and was made more accessible by the construction of the railway line in 1894.

By the time the train reached the town of Vryburg, Daisy and Ethel knew that they were more than half way to Mafeking. Even though it was September, and therefore spring, there was not a whiff of a breeze, and the heat wafting from the station into the compartment felt oppressive.

"Thankfully we should be in Mafeking in another few hours," remarked Ethel, as they settled down again in the carriage, glancing at the dry, rocky landscape as the train pulled out of the station.

Shortly after leaving Vryburg their journey became nerve-racking. Intermittently they could hear the thunder of guns in the distance, reminding them that the railway lines were in constant danger of being sabotaged by the Boers. Two trainloads of women and children passed by, bound for the safety of Cape Town, both travelling from the very area to which they were heading.

Daisy peered out of the window as the train slowed to a stop at the Mafeking railway station. What lay ahead of them, she wondered, as they alighted from the train. A horse drawn carriage took them to the Salvation Army hall, where they wasted no time in unpacking their belongings in the small room attached to the hall, that would be their new home. Their first task would be to contact their fellow Salvationists, who had been without an Officer for some time.

Taking a walk along the main street, they looked about them with interest. The single storey houses, built of unbaked adobe bricks made with the red clay from the brickfields in the town, had corrugated iron roofs. The dusty streets, laid out in a square pattern, had earned Mafeking the nick-name of 'The Biscuit Tin,' for it was hardly attractive. There were schools, a courthouse and gaol, a bank, hotels, a racecourse and recreational ground, a library, churches, a Masonic hall and a few shops.

The Malopo River ran through the town, passing through the brickfields and the African Fingo Village to the south, and another village, occupied by the cattle-keeping Baralong tribe, numbering six thousand, to the west. Their mud huts, scattered on either side of the river, covered a much larger area than the section housing the white settlers. Between the market place and the cemetery stood the hospital and the Catholic Convent, the only two-storey buildings in the town, while opposite the market to the west was the British South African Police Force. Mafeking was an important junction for the railway line running north from Cape Town, thus when the line was extended in 1894 to Bulawayo in Rhodesia, the railway workshops remained there.

The main street was a hub of activity, with horse drawn carts laden with supplies of food and wood. People hurried from one small shop to the next, gathering in whatever they thought would be useful should the Boers besiege the town.

Men busied themselves digging trenches in the back yards of the houses, to be used as dugout shelters if necessary. There were reports that the Boers were gathering on the Transvaal's western border. This prompted refugees, both white and black, to hurry into Mafeking from surrounding farms, seeking shelter from the advancing Boers.

In June 1899, Britain, sensing that war with the Boers was imminent, decided to send Colonel Baden-Powell to Southern Africa to raise two regiments of mounted infantry and train them. He arrived in July, with orders to take charge of the Rhodesian and Bechuanaland Police and organize the defence of these two frontiers. He was told to act discreetly so as not to antagonize the enemy, and where possible to distract them and keep them separated from their own main forces.

Colonel Baden-Powell was considered ideal for the task. He was the son of an Oxford Professor and his mother was the daughter of Admiral W.H. Smyth. He was educated at Charterhouse, after which he decided upon the military as a career. He was known as a good horseman, had an excellent knowledge of topography and small arms, and his military experience included service in Afghanistan, India and Africa.

By the end of September he had organized his two regiments, had them fully trained in the tactics they would be required to use, and was assisted by a group of Officers experienced in local conditions. They also had some knowledge of the Boers and the African tribes living in the area around Mafeking.

He had chosen Mafeking as his base for strategic reasons. Situated on the border of Bechuanaland and the Boer Republics of the Transvaal, it was half way between Rhodesia and the Cape Colony and was 900 miles north of Cape Town. The railway line was a vital link between the two areas.

Knowing that his troops would be severely outnumbered in the field, where the Boer Commandos were better equipped and more experienced in the surrounding terrain, he wisely decided to keep them in Mafeking. He would have to use his ingenuity to convert Mafeking into a town capable of withstanding a Boer attack, with the limited resources available to him. Baden-Powell's request for adequate artillery had been disregarded and he had less than he required.

When the threat of war grew, Baden—Powell brought an armed force—his entire garrison—into Mafeking in September, to guard the stores that had been brought in by rail. He stockpiled large supplies of food, hay for the horses and railroad equipment and took over the office of Mr. Minchin, the local lawyer, for use as part of his headquarters. On the roof was a lookout post, equipped with a speaking tube and protected with sandbags, while below were screened living quarters. He ordered the erection of several small forts, linked by field telephone to his headquarters at Dixon's Hotel, which were next to Mr. Minchin's office. He also made use of an armoured train, on a hastily constructed railway line, equipped with arms and ammunition, that proved a mobile and effective weapon in the months to come.

After meeting up with local Salvationists at their hall, Daisy and Ethel walked around the town to familiarize themselves with the layout, and stopped frequently to speak to the inhabitants.

Although many women and children had already been sent out of Mafeking to safer areas, about six hundred still remained, mainly the families of approximately a thousand men protecting the town. They were reluctant to leave their menfolk. Others had come in from surrounding farms, seeking protection. Those women whose homes were near the edge of the town and therefore in danger of being hit by Boer shells, moved into other houses near the centre of the town. Others camped out in their covered wagons, under which a trench was dug to provide shelter should the enemy shells reach that part of the town.

Willie and Ada Cock, well known farmers in the area, were among those seeking refuge. They ran the cattle ranch Oaklands, seven miles outside Mafeking, for Ada's sister Emily and brother-in-law Harry Fuller. Travelling in their covered wagon with their four children, they arrived in the town on October 3rd, bringing with them their herd of cattle, a mare with a foal, a goat and some fowl. They moved into a small house on the banks of the Malopo River.

Colonel Baden-Powell appeared confident that the siege, if it were to happen as expected, would last for only a few weeks, at which time British reinforcements would arrive to relieve them and the Boers would retreat. Even though Baden-Powell's forces were heavily outnumbered, he felt his battalion could protect the town until their arrival.

Mafeking was swarming with soldiers, gathering materials to reinforce the defences on the perimeter of the town. One Sergeant, on noting the arrival of Daisy and Ethel, dressed in their Salvation Army uniforms, stopped and spoke to them.

"Who sent you here?" he demanded, "Don't you know that Mafeking is in danger of being besieged? This is no place for two young women!"

"We've come to help our fellow Salvationists," Daisy replied firmly. "We can't leave them at a time like this without an Officer. Besides, we could be of use to you and the residents as well. We are not afraid of the danger."

"Well, I don't think it is wise for you to remain here. You should leave Mafeking while there is still time," he advised, before hurrying off to help with the fortifications.

Disregarding his advice, Daisy and Ethel returned to the Salvation Army office and continued contacting the Salvationists on their list. They were soon involved in helping to prepare safer shelters in the centre of the town, where, hopefully, the Boer shells would be unable to reach.

On October 9th President Paul Kruger issued a forty-eight hour ultimatum to the British to withdraw their troops, and when that expired, they declared war on the British. The Second Boer War had begun, on October 11th, 1899.

Altogether, the Boers had at their command thirty-five thousand men against fifteen thousand British troops, and felt confident of their ability. They were superb horsemen, armed with modern clip-loading Mauser rifles, and were experienced marksmen, able to operate freely in their own familiar territory.

Carrying dried strips of meat, called biltong, and rusks, dried bread, to satisfy their hunger, they were able to hide out in the rugged terrain without being easily observed, because their khaki clothing blended with the dusty veld (grassland).

The British soldiers, by contrast, were at a disadvantage in unfamiliar surroundings and were unable to understand the local African languages spoken by the Fingoes and the Baralongs.

When desperate fighting broke out a few miles from Mafeking, the residents were on edge all night, hardly daring to sleep. The Boers could surround the town at any time, making it difficult for the British soldiers to keep in contact with the rest of the forces.

Early in the morning of October 12th, the soldiers hastily assisted a trainload of women and children to leave the town, bound for the safety of Cape Town. With the Boers closing in, Colonel Baden-Powell issued an order that all remaining women and children were to depart at once. However, he made an exception to allow some of the army officers' wives to stay with them, along with some young boys between the ages of nine and fifteen, who were reluctant to leave their parents.

To their dismay, Daisy and Ethel were also ordered to leave Mafeking. In vain they pleaded to be allowed to remain, but the military authorities were adamant.

"The Colonel has ordered all women and children to be evacuated from the town, Captain," one of the Sergeants told Daisy, "There could be heavy fighting and your lives will be in danger. There will be only two more trains leaving today. Gather your belongings and leave at once!"

"At least let us help the women and children to get safely onto the trains," Daisy pleaded, "We'll leave on the last train today."

Daisy and Ethel spent the day helping to carry the luggage of the women and children, soothing the frightened, sobbing mothers bidding their husbands farewell and helping them to get settled on the trains. Soldiers urged the passengers to hurry. There was no time to waste.

"You must leave now, Captain," urged one army officer, addressing Daisy, "Colonel Baden-Powell wants his orders carried out. Women and children are to leave as quickly as possible."

Eventually Daisy and Ethel found time to hurry back to the Salvation Army Hall, where they hastily packed a small suitcase each, leaving their heavy trunks in the hall.

Winding their way through the throng of people on the platform of the railway station they boarded the train and managed to find seats in a crowded compartment. With sinking hearts they watched Mafeking fade in the distance as the train began its long journey to Cape Town through the hot semi-desert of the Karroo. How would those poor inhabitants who had been left behind in Mafeking fare against a Boer attack, they wondered, and would Colonel Baden-Powell and his troops be able to protect them?

The train journey was tense, with crying children clinging to their mothers, who tried to soothe them. Daisy and Ethel did their best to help the mothers on the long, monotonous journey, broken only by occasional half—hour restaurant stops at various stations. As there was little to choose from on the menu, most people ordered soup, which since it was served piping hot, was a challenge to finish before the train pulled out of the station again.

At length the train stopped at a small station called Three Sisters, where a distressing sight greeted their gaze. A short distance further on, sprawled on their sides, were several derailed railway coaches of the train that had left Mafeking before them. The most damaged coach looked as though it had been sawn in half. Seven people—women and children—had lost their lives.

Railway workers hurried about, searching through the wreckage and surveying the damage caused by the Boers sabotaging the railway line.

Daisy shivered. Earlier that day they had helped those same passengers to board the train, and had been urged to board it themselves. By travelling on the later train their own lives had been spared. They had indeed been guided into taking the last train out of Mafeking!

CHAPTER 13

THE BOERS BESIEGE MAFEKING

Because of the derailment at Three Sisters, the train on which Daisy and Ethel were travelling was delayed for several hours, and it was therefore almost two days before it eventually puffed into Cape Town's railway station, to the relief of its weary passengers. They had at last reached the safety of the Cape Peninsula.

From there it was a short train ride to Observatory, where the Stevens family lived. They were surprised to see them.

"Thank heavens you're back, safe and sound!" exclaimed Mr. Stevens, as he and his wife hugged Ethel and Daisy.

"We're so relieved you're here," added Mrs. Stevens, "because we heard of the derailment at Three Sisters, and we were under the impression that you were travelling on that train."

"Fortunately we were on the train that left after that one, Mother," said Ethel, "but so much has happened since we left Mafeking that we will need to catch up with the news."

Events had unfolded rapidly, Daisy and Ethel learned, when they read the newspaper reports at the Stevens' home. It appeared that yet another train had been sent from Mafeking, taking women and children to safety. Leaving several hours after the one on which Daisy and Ethel were travelling, it was intercepted by a Boer patrol and turned back to Mafeking, arriving back in the town the next day.

"I'm surprised that another train left after ours, commented Ethel, "as I thought that we were on the last train out of Mafeking."

"It appears that we were," replied Daisy, "as the next train had to return to the town."

"Did you hear about Lady Sarah Wilson?" asked Ethel, "Her husband commanded a company in Mafeking. She was very reluctant to leave Mafeking because her husband was stationed there, but was ordered by the Colonel Commanding to go."

Lady Sarah, an aunt of Winston Churchill, was a strong, formidable woman. The Duke of Marlborough's daughter, she had grown up in the luxury of Blenheim Palace in England. She was also a newspaper correspondent for the *London Daily Mail* and was married to Captain Gordon Wilson of the Royal Horse Guards. On a visit from England to Cape Town at Christmas 1895, they stayed with Cecil John Rhodes in his then unfinished Groote Schuur mansion and associated with the wealthy diamond merchants of Kimberley.

They returned to England but came back to South Africa four months before the outbreak of the Boer War, and while in Cape Town they met Colonel Baden-Powell. Captain Wilson became his aide-de-camp and was sent, along with Lady Sarah, to Bulawayo in Rhodesia to await the inevitable war.

Upon arrival in Mafeking Lady Sarah selected a site in the centre of the town where she erected a tent above a dugout and furnished it very comfortably. She was intent on staying there should the town be besieged.

Colonel Baden-Powell, however, not wishing to have the responsibility of caring for her in the event of a siege, sent her away for safety to James Keely's farm at Mosita in the Northern Cape, where the red sands of the Kalahari desert begin. The farm was near the settlement of Setlogoli, situated half way between Vryburg and Mafeking.

It was now October 14th. The Boers had cut the telephone lines, making it impossible to send off any messages; but the British soldiers were undeterred. They let loose a batch of carrier pigeons, bearing notes attached to their legs, which flew straight to the town of Kimberley. Soon the world received the news that Mafeking, under the command of Colonel Baden-Powell, was under siege.

On that same day, October 14th 1899, Boer Commandos besieged Kimberley. The British forces, trying to prevent the siege, suffered severe losses.

Daisy, knowing that her family in England would be anxious about her, sent them a telegram, reassuring them that she and Ethel were safely back in Cape Town, with the Stevens family.

After a few days of rest, Daisy was ready to report to the Commissioner at the Salvation Army Headquarters in Cape Town, where she was greeted with a chilly reception.

"According to the newspapers, the nuns at the Catholic Convent remained in Mafeking—but the Salvation Army Officers left! What reason did you have for deserting your post?" the Commissioner demanded.

"We had no option but to leave, Commissioner Kilby," she explained. "The Sergeant in charge refused to allow us to stay, even though we begged him."

"Well, I am most disappointed that you did not stay on. As soon as the siege is over—and hopefully that will be soon—you will be sent back to your post in Mafeking."

Daisy bit back a retort. How could the Commissioner expect her to defy the British Army? Besides, she was also responsible for Ethel's safety.

Cape Town, securely under the control of the British, was a safe area and was relatively untouched by the conflict. However, the residents knew that the outcome of the war would have an impact on them as well.

In the meantime Daisy was given the task of running the "Young Soldier," a newspaper for children. Delighted with this new job at Headquarters, she would sit at the window and gaze across at Table Mountain, "chewing stories out of her lead pencil." Always having been interested in writing, her communication skills would be put to good use. One of the songs she composed in 1900 was as follows:

Lord, we praise Thee for the blessings
Which Thou hast on us bestowed,
Now our heartfelt thanks we render
For the kindness Thou hast shewed.
Make us thankful
For Thy mercies great and good.
Precious Saviour, wilt Thou make us
Pure and spotless in Thy sight,
So that dying souls around us,
We may lead into the light?
Make us holy,
Let Thy will be our delight.
On Thy promises we're standing,
Trusting Thee we cannot fail;
With Thy boundless grace upholding,
In Thy strength we must prevail.
Make us conquerors
Though a host of foes assail.

During Self Denial, a period when an all-out effort was made to collect funds for the Salvation Army's work, Daisy was sent to the nearby town of Wellington to help the officer there, a young German woman whose brothers were helping the Boers upcountry in their fight against the British. However, politics played no part in the work of the Salvation Army.

Most of the inhabitants of Wellington were Dutch, with High Dutch being the language used in their schools and in the Dutch Reformed Churches. Being fluent in the language, Daisy's companion proved to be an invaluable asset.

Daisy had left eagerly on this mission, for it provided an opportunity for her to see another part of the beautiful Cape Province. From Wellington they journeyed on to the two picturesque towns of Ceres and Tulbach, walking for miles from farm to farm, and stopping at intervals to rest and admire the towering mountains and sparkling streams, as well as the huge vineyards and orchards.

As hospitable as ever, the Dutch farmers offered them peaches and grapes and told them to take as much fruit as they wanted, and one kind hearted elderly lady in Tulbach provided them with accommodation for the night.

"Just look at this huge feather bed!" Daisy exclaimed in delight. "It's so high that we'll have to use a chair to climb up onto it! We're sure to have a good night's sleep."

Collecting funds in Tulbach proved to be a pleasure. The little town, with its quaint, white washed Cape Dutch houses and beautiful shady trees, had mountain water running down the open gutters in the streets. Yet despite all the beauty and tranquillity around them, Daisy was very aware of the war raging in many parts of South Africa, and prayed for a peaceful settlement.

On Daisy's return to Cape Town, Walter's sister contacted her and invited her to lunch, where she had a joyful reunion with Walter. In the weeks that followed, Daisy became a frequent visitor to their home, the family carefully arranging things so that Daisy and Walter were able to spend time together.

One Saturday afternoon the family went walking on Signal Hill overlooking Cape Town. It was a beautiful, warm summer day, with wild flowers dotting the hillside and wisps of cotton wool clouds draped over Table Mountain. On such a perfect day it felt good to be alive.

On their descent Walter's sister hurried the children on ahead, leaving Walter alone with Daisy. This was the opportunity for which he had been waiting.

"Soon I'll be leaving for the Orange River to work amongst the troops, Daisy," he told her, "and it might be many months before we are able to meet again. I'd feel much happier about going if you would agree to become engaged to me."

Daisy's eyes were shining as she gazed into his handsome face, so close to her own.

"Yes, Walter, this time I would love to accept your proposal," she replied, sealing her promise with a tender kiss.

That evening they announced their engagement to Walter's family, who welcomed the news. During the time they had spent in Daisy's company they had grown to love her, and felt that she would make a good wife for Walter.

"I'm glad you weren't allowed to stay on in Mafeking," Walter remarked. "We would have been parted for so long, and I would have been worried about you."

"I still feel disappointed, though, that Colonel Baden-Powell insisted on us leaving Mafeking. We could have helped the people trapped in the town. I wonder what became of Mrs. Ada Cock and her children, and the other women and children who were forced to return to Mafeking when the last train was turned back by the Boers," Daisy said thoughtfully.

"We should know soon enough," Walter replied, "because more British troops are being sent to South Africa, so the siege will probably not last much longer."

But the Boers proved to be much more difficult to defeat than the British had imagined, and the war dragged on, with thousands of casualties on both sides.

Under this cloud of uncertainty Walter and Daisy pondered their future, wondering when it would be possible for them to marry.

CHAPTER 14

COPING WITH LIFE UNDER SIEGE

Since Daisy's return to Cape Town the newspapers had been full of the news of the Boer War, raging in the Provinces of the Transvaal and the Orange Free State. Mafeking was still under siege, but messages were smuggled out of the town in various ways. African messengers, who were well paid, were used to smuggle out letters and news reports. Some hid messages in the soles of their shoes and ran under cover of darkness along the banks of the Malopo River, generally managing to evade the Boers. Some went south, others north, passing through the Boer cordon surrounding the town. Many of the runners took letters and news reports to the postal authorities in Bechuanaland, from where the news reached the outside world.

The Boers besieged the town of Kimberley in the Northern Cape, on October 14th, 1899, trapping Cecil John Rhodes, the mining magnate, in the town. Then, on November 2nd, 1899, the Boers besieged the town of Ladysmith as well.

Winston Churchill, a young newspaper correspondent for the *Morning Post* in England, and nephew of Lady Sarah, was captured in Pretoria by the Boers and locked in a Pretoria prison. He managed to escape through the roof, climbed onto a railway bridge and jumped onto a passing freight train, and returned to the troops to cover the war.

British troops from Australia, New Zealand and Canada, arriving by ship in Cape Town, had to disperse to different parts of the country to counteract the Boer attacks. Baden-Powell, under siege in Mafeking, found his hopes fading for a quick relief by the British forces.

The Boers acquired a 'Long Tom' Creosot 94-pounder gun, with which they periodically pounded Mafeking. Nick-named 'Old Creaky,' it caused some damage to buildings in the town and sent the local people scurrying into their trenches. The Boers also aimed it frequently at the women's laager, namely the covered wagons under which trenches had been dug, as well as at the Victoria Hospital.

The Boer War dragged on, week after week, with Baden-Powell using all his ingenuity to outwit the Boers, who easily outnumbered his own soldiers. He set up look-out posts in strategic places in the town, and tricked the Boers by laying a railway track and placing a carriage laden with explosives on it. When the Boers attacked it, there was a terrific explosion and they suffered a severe setback. He also tricked them into believing that they had laid several land mines around the outskirts of the town, thus making the Boers wary of trying to infiltrate it.

The Boers discovered that Lady Sarah Wilson was living on Keeley's farm and went to investigate, suspecting that she was a British spy. But Lady Sarah managed to evade them and sought refuge with a Scottish couple, the Frasers, who owned the store at Setlagoli.

By then the town of Vryburg had fallen into the hands of the Boers, who occupied Setlagoli as well. Lady Sarah was taken prisoner, but because the Boers didn't know what to do with her, they told her to remain with the Frasers until further notice. They then galloped down the dusty road to the Keeley's farm and burned down their house, leaving Mrs. Keeley and her six children homeless.

Lady Sarah, bored with the inactivity at Setlagoli, informed the Boers that she wished to rejoin her husband in Mafeking. She told the Boer commander, General Cronje, that the Frasers had no more food and she wished to return to Mafeking. After negotiations with Colonel

Baden-Powell, it was agreed that she would be exchanged for one of their prisoners, Petrus Viljoen, a spy and convicted horse thief.

Back in Mafeking, her news reports of events in Mafeking were smuggled out and were published regularly overseas. Her comparatively luxurious dugout became a focal point for social events, and before long she was in charge of the auxiliary hospital that had been established to cope with dysentery, malaria and typhoid. Many of the injured soldiers died from these diseases.

Although food and supplies had been stockpiled in the town in anticipation of a siege, they began to dwindle as time went by, and food rationing had to be implemented. Noting that the nurses and orderlies were working exhausting hours, she insisted that they be given special rations. Eventually the nuns from the Roman Catholic Convent took over the running of the hospital.

At the dawn of the 20th century there was still no sign of the awaited British troops. The Boers shelled the town relentlessly, forcing the women and children to retreat into their dugouts, where they spent the whole of New Year's Day.

The houses in the town were built low and made of mud brick, with tin roofs, thus the Boer shells pounded right through the brick walls. Whenever shelling commenced the soldiers notified the residents with a siren, to warn them to get into their trenches.

The Baralongs, themselves running short of food, began night raids on the cattle belonging to the Boers. Being dark skinned, and wearing very little clothing, they were difficult to detect as they crept along the banks of the river at night. Their experience with handling cattle was so useful that they were able to steal some of them and drive them back into the town. When that happened there was much rejoicing among the Baralongs, who celebrated their victory with songs and dances.

Months went by, with the food shortage becoming critical. The Africans were so hungry that they resorted to eating dogs, and when a swarm of locusts descended upon the town, they pounced on them and ate them. Many of the white people ate the locusts as well, after roasting them.

The Boers were intent on starving the residents of the town into surrender, but Baden-Powell held onto the hope that the British forces would soon relieve the town, and stubbornly resisted surrendering to the Boers.

As conditions worsened he ordered several horses to be shot at intervals, thus supplying the people in the town with a little meat, to supplement the meagre diet of the food supplied by the town's grocer, Mr. Weil. At times the residents were obliged to exist on two biscuits a day, which the residents referred to as 'dog biscuits.'

Baden-Powell ordered the town's printer to print Mafeking Siege Notes, the currency being to the value of one pound and ten shillings, as well as postage stamps bearing the words 'Mafeking besieged.' The currency would be exchanged for coin on resumption of civil law at the Standard Bank, Mafeking, when the town was relieved. The *Mafeking Mail* was printed as usual, carrying news of the events in the town and elsewhere.

This was a so-called 'Gentlemen's War' with the cessation of hostilities every Sunday, when each side would retire to church services. At times, on a Sunday, there would even be a peaceful meeting of the leaders of both sides at the outposts!

Because each side refrained from firing on a Sunday, Baden-Powell organized various social events to keep up the morale of the inhabitants. A Siege Exhibition was held, where prizes were awarded for fine handiwork, including Irish lace, embroidery, woodwork, paintings, essays and musical compositions. Mrs. Ada Cock was awarded a prize of five pounds for her composition of a waltz.

There were also sports days where horsemen would dress up in clown costumes and race around the football field, much to the amusement of the onlookers. Baden-Powell also arranged cricket and football matches, pony racing and polo, as well as Sunday concerts. The

Boers, sitting on the banks of their trenches, watched through their field glasses, no doubt amazed at the resilience of the inhabitants.

However, on Monday mornings the Boers resumed the shelling of the town. Casualties mounted on both sides, with many wounded or killed. About thirty-three young boys, members of the Cadet Messenger Corps, bravely carried messages from Colonel Baden-Powell in his look-out post at Dixon's Hotel to soldiers in the field, providing invaluable information. They also kept a lookout on the Boer forces, warning the residents when they saw signs of the Boers loading their cannons, and helped the hospital staff by running errands. Dressed in their khaki uniforms and wide brimmed hats turned up on the left side, they inspired Colonel Baden-Powell to start the Boy Scouts movement seven years later in England.

Nurse Crawford and Mrs. Buchan carried medical supplies and food to the captive Officers and wounded Boers in Colonel Hore's fort, while under heavy fire from both sides. There were numerous acts of bravery and compassion during this long, drawn-out siege.

In one of a series of letters to her sister, which were smuggled out of the town, Ada Cock described how she was awakened at 5 a.m. and asked to go and deliver the baby of Mrs. Minchen, because the doctor was unable to attend to her. She delivered a healthy baby, taking this event in her stride.

On February 15th, 1900 the siege of Kimberley came to an end when British regiments arrived and forced the Boers to retreat. This gave Mafeking residents new hope.

Shortly thereafter the siege of Ladysmith came to an end on February 27th, 1900, when British troops under General Buller relieved the town after fierce fighting. The Boers retreated, much to the relief of the inhabitants, who were suffering from a shortage of food.

Daisy and Walter, closely following events, prepared themselves for whatever they would be called upon to do. Knowing that she would be sent back to Mafeking when the siege ended, Daisy wondered how much longer it would be before it was safe to return.

According to reports coming from Mafeking, as the months dragged by, the people were becoming desperate for food. The Africans were shooting all the dogs and eating them, to supplement their meagre rations of maize meal, and the white inhabitants were eating horses and donkeys in order to survive. There were heavy casualties among the soldiers and civilians, with many deaths due to typhoid, dysentery and malaria.

Ada Cock carefully guarded her cow, well aware of how precious its milk was to her children, who were becoming thin and sickly. One of their cows had already been stolen, and they couldn't afford to lose another. Many of the children in the town had died of malnutrition and disease.

It was now the beginning of May, 1900. Their rations consisted of biscuits, oat buns and horse sausage, and the supply was running out. If the British forces did not arrive soon, there would be many more deaths. All they could do was live in hope that Mafeking would soon be relieved.

Then, on May 16th, 1900, the whole situation changed, causing much excitement and hope among the besieged inhabitants. Colonel Plumer's forces met up with Colonel Mahon's relief forces about nineteen miles outside of Mafeking, where they waited for the Royal Canadian Artillery to join them. Fighting their way through, they reached the outskirts of Mafeking and stopped to rest overnight before their final onslaught on the Boer forces, planned for the following day.

Then, at dusk, Major Karri Davis with a twelve-man patrol of the Imperial Light Horse (an exceptionally efficient force originally raised among British refugees from the Transvaal), rode into the town, after travelling over the waterless desert for two days following sandy tracks, and covering twenty-two miles per day. At 3 a.m. on the morning of May 17th, many more soldiers marched in, bringing with them fifty-two mule wagons with ten mules to each, carrying supplies. The force now consisted of twelve hundred men. Among them were the Royal Canadian Field Artillery, Canadian Light Horse, Royal Canadian

Mounted Rifles, Royal Canadian Dragoons and Gordon Highlanders. Accompanying them were the Queensland Mounted Infantry and the Maxim Gun Company of Australia and New Zealand Imperial Bushmen. The local people watched with nervousness and excitement, fervently hoping that the Boers would be driven away and the siege lifted.

CHAPTER 15

JUBILANT SCENES AS MAFEKING IS RELIEVED

Early in the morning of May 17th, 1900, a fierce battle commenced between the British and the Boers, which the local residents watched from whatever vantage point they could find. Many of them climbed onto the roof of a nearby house. After several hours of fighting, during which both sides suffered heavy casualties, the British horsemen rode full tilt from both sides towards the Boer laager, and succeeded in forcing the Boers to make a hasty retreat, leaving behind their wagons loaded with food. Mafeking, after being under siege for two hundred and seventeen days, had been relieved!

There were scenes of wild rejoicing in the town, as the victorious troops marched into the market square, playing their bugles, drums and bagpipes. People danced and sang 'Goodbye, Dolly Gray,' a popular song in 1900, waved British flags and congratulated the troops.

For the first time in seven months the residents were able to walk in the streets without fear of being hit by a Boer shell. Soon a train from Bulawayo in Rhodesia would be arriving with food—none too soon for the weak, hungry inhabitants. And, thankfully, they would be able to enjoy a long soak in a bath—a luxury they had been denied for several months during the heavy shelling.

As word spread about the ending of the siege, residents of Cape Town began celebrating, decorating the streets with bunting. Singing, chanting crowds danced in the streets, far into the night.

In Britain wild excitement greeted the news. Men and women wept with relief, seemingly delirious with joy. Seething crowds thronged the streets of London all night, giving vent to their elation. They waved thousands of flags, church bells rang and steamboats on the River Thames whistled enthusiastically.

Twenty thousand people crowded into the grounds of Mansion House, where Colonel Baden-Powell's portrait was on display. The Lord Mayor, speaking from the balcony, said he wished the cheers could reach Mafeking.

Ten thousand people serenaded Colonel Baden-Powell's mother, proclaiming her son as the 'Hero of the Hour,' and at places of amusement there were scenes of frenzied rejoicing. Canada, Australia, New Zealand and the United States of America were wildly enthusiastic and hundreds of congratulatory messages were cabled to Mafeking.

Daisy, in a post card to her mother, wrote:

> *My dearest Mother,*
> *I'm quite happy, especially now that Mafeking has been relieved. I long to be there. Keep believing,*
> *Daisy.*

For Daisy, the news meant one thing: the way would soon be open for her to return to her post in Mafeking to resume the work she had originally been sent to do.

However, because the war was far from over, with Boer patrols still operating in various parts of the country, and it was dangerous and difficult to travel between the main towns, permits would have to be obtained to enter certain areas. The Commissioner therefore decided to send Daisy in company with some other Officers as far as Kimberley, from where a permit would be applied for to enable her to continue her journey to Mafeking. Accommodation in Kimberley would also have to be arranged before Daisy and other Officers could leave.

Eventually the long awaited permits arrived, enabling Daisy and her companions to travel from Cape Town to Kimberley, from where all the Officers would be sent back to their posts once they had obtained the necessary travel permits in Kimberley.

Once again Daisy found herself on a train bound for Kimberley, this time accompanied by Lieutenant Cullinan (related to the family who later found fame through diamond mining). Also in their party of Officers was the young Lieutenant Adam Barnard, who was posted at the seaside town of Knysna. (Years later his son, Dr. Christiaan Barnard, would become a surgeon and perform the world's first heart transplant at Groote Schuur Hospital in Cape Town). He did not stay long, however, because he suffered from ill health and returned to Knysna. He eventually became a minister in the Dutch Reformed Church and worked among the Coloured community in Beaufort West.

While awaiting their permits they all lived in a boarding house and assisted with the work in the town. During the siege some of the buildings in Kimberley had been damaged and the hospital staff was kept busy tending to those injured in the fighting. Although the siege had been lifted three months earlier, many of the injured had remained for treatment.

The young Officers were soon involved in helping the inhabitants wherever they could, and listened to accounts of how dangerous and difficult life had been for the beleaguered residents of Kimberley. There had been 1,500 deaths, mainly due to typhoid fever, and many of them were babies and children. People had stood in a line for over three hours waiting for their turn to receive a little horse meat or soup, all the while hoping they would not be hit by a shell.

The situation had worsened when the Boers started using one hundred pound shells from their newly acquired Long Tom gun, forcing the residents to seek shelter under the bridge or in the mine shaft for four days and nights.

Food was slow in reaching the town at the end of the siege, therefore many of the residents who were able to leave boarded trains to Cape Town, to rest and recover physically from their hardships.

Eventually the long awaited permits arrived in Kimberley, enabling Daisy and Lieutenant Cullinan to make plans for their departure to Mafeking.

"I can't believe I'll be back in Mafeking soon!" Daisy exclaimed excitedly. "I had to leave the town eight months ago, and so much has happened there since then."

"We'll need to take a good supply of food with us, because they are sure to be short of all sorts of things," replied the practical Lieutenant Cullinan, as they began stocking up on food and blankets, pillows and cutlery, ready for their train journey to Mafeking.

Daisy, packing up yet once again, wondered what lay ahead of them in this war-torn part of the country.

CHAPTER 16

DAISY RETURNS TO MAFEKING

On their arrival in Mafeking they found that many of the buildings had been badly damaged, with the Salvation Army hall receiving its fair share of Boer shells.

"Look at those holes in the walls!" gasped Daisy, staring in awe at the damage to the hall. Remembering how hot it had been in the summer during her short stay before the siege, she smiled wryly and added: "At least the holes will let in some cool fresh air." Entering the room attached to it, which had been her bedroom, she picked her way gingerly through the debris on the ground, expecting to find the worst. When she and Ethel Stevens had left the town they had been forced to leave behind their tin trunks, containing many of their personal belongings. Now they were buried beneath a mound of bricks and wood.

"My framed Commission was on the wall of this little room, and now it is buried under all this rubble," she commented, as a wave of despair swept over her. "That Commission meant a lot to me. I kept it in sight to remind me of the days when I was a young rebel, and how my life was changed when I became converted."

Raking feverishly among the ruins, Daisy at last uncovered her tin trunk and opened it to inspect the damage. A shell had gone right through it, ruining many of the contents, including her Bible, which had a hole right through the centre. Nearby, miraculously undamaged except for a broken glass and a few scratches on the wooden frame, was her Commission. She scooped it up in delight and resolved to nail it to the wall of their new quarters.

While they were examining the hall the shy young Secretary of the Corps, Tommy Young, joined them and informed them that ammunition had been stored under the platform in the hall but had now been removed. They both breathed a sigh of relief.

"Let me take you to your new quarters, Captain," he suggested, leading the way to a small, semi-detached house nearby. On the door was chalked a message: 'Open gently or the roof will fall in.'

Noting her hesitation, he laughed.

"Don't worry about that notice," he advised, "it was written during the siege, but the house has been repaired since then. It's quite safe."

Daisy and Lieutenant Cullinan inspected their new home. The floor was made of layers of mud taken from anthills, a common practice in those days, and above the cracked walls was a calico ceiling. The bedroom contained three rough packing cases for use as a dresser and chair, two iron bedsteads and a small table.

The kitchen had a fireplace but no stove, and in one corner of the room stood a food chest, its large wooden frame covered with a fine chicken netting. Next to it was a large box of groceries that the Secretary had thoughtfully provided for them.

After Tommy Young had departed, Daisy began to unpack the groceries.

"I'm so tired," she sighed, sinking down onto a packing case that served as a chair, "and I'm dying for a nice cup of tea. If we could find some wood we could start a fire in the fireplace and boil some water."

"Leave that to me, Captain," suggested Lieutenant Cullinan, "I'll see what I can find."

Emptying the remainder of the groceries onto the table she took the wooden box outside, and after having persuaded an old woman down the road to lend her an axe, she soon had enough wood to start a fire.

Meanwhile, Daisy went to the store nearby and bought some matting to put on the bedroom floor, and set about making the little cottage as comfortable as possible.

That night Daisy awoke to feel a tingling, itching sensation all over her body. Hurriedly lighting her candle next to her bed, she discovered that the bed was crawling with hundreds of little black ants! Wearily the two young women got up to wage war on the unwelcome intruders, which had been attracted in the first place by the groceries.

The next morning they discovered to their disgust that not only had they been visited by black ants, but that white ants had eaten a large hole in the new matting.

"There's only one way to keep the ants at bay," declared Lieutenant Cullinan, "and that is to stand the legs of the food chest in tins of water."

Daisy was grateful for the resourcefulness of Lieutenant Cullinan. She could turn her hand to almost anything, and when on one occasion they were given an ostrich egg, she made a milk tart with it, baking it in a three legged pot over the fire. She could also speak Fingoe, the language of the African people in the village, which made communication with them easier.

The two young women were soon made to feel welcome in the small community of Mafeking. When the pay train came in, bringing the groceries ordered by the men working on the railways, they would find a pile of groceries placed on the table in the hall, for the men always ordered a little extra for them.

One elderly woman who owned a cow supplied them with a gallon of milk a day. Not wishing to refuse her generosity, they accepted it and passed on what they did not need to some of the railway men who suffered periodic bouts of malaria that they had contracted while working in Rhodesia. Often they sent soup too, for which the men were grateful, as they were weak and unable to digest heavy meals.

Daisy soon found that there was so much to do and so many people in need of help in the town. The hospital was full of injured soldiers and civilians, being cared for by the nuns from the Catholic Convent as well as a few nurses and women who had offered their services. Without hesitation Daisy and Lieutenant Cullinan joined them, providing practical help and comfort wherever it was needed. Some of the soldiers, lying in makeshift tent hospitals, were unable to write letters themselves, and asked them to write messages to their anxious families in Britain. Sitting beside injured soldiers they provided friendship and caring, offering up a prayer for their recovery. Seeing the grateful smiles on their faces was reward enough for the two young Salvation Army Officers.

Meetings in the Salvation Army Hall were usually well attended by soldiers and the railway men, who treated Daisy and Lieutenant Cullinan with respect and affection. There were very few women in the town, for most of the evacuees had not yet returned, preferring to remain with their children in safer areas. As well, many of their homes had been damaged by the Boer shells and needed repairs.

"Do you know what became of Mrs. Ada Cock?" Daisy enquired of Tommy Young.

"Mrs. Cock left recently for their farm, Oaklands. Her husband Willie went off with General Hunter's column, as they needed him as a guide. During the siege most of their cattle were used for food, with only two cows being spared for their milk. But by the time she left there was only one cow, because the other had been stolen for food."

"And where is Lady Sarah Wilson now?" was Daisy's next question.

"Lady Sarah left shortly after the siege ended," Tommy Young replied, "and she probably went to Cape Town. No doubt she will return to England soon. Colonel Baden-Powell also left, to continue his war service in some other part of the country."

Daisy and Lieutenant Cullinan often held open—air meetings in the evenings, usually under a lamp post that provided enough light to read the song books. When there was no convenient light, one of the men, usually old Tom, would hold up a paraffin lamp. Invariably he held it on the wrong side of the wind, causing those present to cough and splutter from the fumes.

"Isn't he a Silly Billy!" Daisy would exclaim in exasperation after the meeting. "Every Corps seems to have one. And yet, what would we do without them?"

One evening the wind sprang up, howling through the holes in the hall. Eventually it succeeded in blowing out the lights in the paraffin lamps suspended from the ceiling, and the meeting had to be cancelled.

A few weeks later the wind played further havoc—this time of a much more serious nature. Tommy Young had barely reached their cottage to check their set of books, when great gusts of wind began to rattle the window panes and doors, howling around the corners of the building and swirling up the dust.

In the distance a rumble of thunder could be heard, followed by a blinding flash of lightning. The little house shook. Daisy glanced uneasily at her companions. Seconds later there was a thunderous crash. The house shook again—violently—as though in the grip of an earthquake, while the wind kept up its incessant howl.

"Let's barricade the doors!" suggested the Secretary, pushing the heavy packing case against the front door, while Daisy and Lieutenant Cullinan pushed the kitchen table against the back door. With a mighty roar the rain began pelting down relentlessly on the tin roof, making conversation almost impossible.

"You had better spend the night here, Mr. Young!" Daisy yelled above the noise, "You can't possibly go home in such a storm. We'll make up a bed for you on the table."

The storm raged fiercely all night, until at last, with the first flush of dawn, the wind died down almost as suddenly as it had started. When Daisy and Lieutenant Cullinan had dressed they went to inspect the damage. Tommy Young, they discovered, had already departed, having moved the packing cases away from the door.

The sight that met their gaze stunned them. On the ground, a few feet away from their front verandah, rested their neighbour's new roof. Beside their house, spread right across the road, lay a huge bluegum tree, its heavy trunk and branches so close to their house that it had narrowly missed hitting their roof. Daisy bowed her head and prayed silently. God had spared them yet again from harm!

"I wonder how the hall withstood the storm," Lieutenant Cullinan said anxiously. "It could never have survived, especially with all those shell holes in it."

Hurrying to the hall, they found the Secretary already there.

"Well, Captain, the hall wasn't even damaged," he said with relief. "When a cyclone can't get into a building it flattens it. But when the wind struck the wall it was able to rush through those shell holes and spend its force. We can be thankful they were there!"

Daisy, hurrying into the hall, found to her relief that there was very little damage. A note, kept in place by a packet of sugar, caught her attention.

Dear Captain, she read, *thank you for the shelter. We slept here last night.* It was signed by one of the soldiers who had arrived with his Company from the town of Zeerust. The cyclone had flattened their tents, which had been pitched on the banks of the river, and the soldiers had sought shelter in the railway station waiting room and the Salvation Army hall.

It was soon apparent that the cyclone had severely damaged the buildings in the town, causing more damage, in fact, than all the Boer shells. Chimney tops had crashed through roofs, walls had collapsed in heaps of rubble and trees were uprooted. Miraculously, nobody was injured.

The two young women worked tirelessly all day among the troops, helping to arrange temporary accommodation for them among the residents of the town, and providing hot soup and bread.

That evening some of the soldiers turned up to the Salvation Army service in a strange assortment of clothing, borrowed from the local residents, for most of them had lost all their belongings when the storm struck and the normally dry river bed became a raging torrent. One young man appeared in his pajamas and overcoat. After the service he approached Daisy.

"Excuse my appearance, Captain," he said, "but I lost all my clothing last night. And I lost something far more valuable than that too: the Bible my mother gave me before I left to fight in this country. Do you perhaps have a spare one?"

Daisy looked with compassion at the tall young soldier, then she took from her bag the treasured Bible her mother had given her as a parting gift when she left England.

"You shall have my Bible," she said, writing a suitable inscription in it before handing it to him, "and may God go with you."

Daisy never saw the soldier again, for shortly afterwards he was sent back to England. But truth is stranger than fiction. One evening he was testifying at a Salvation Army meeting in London, which by chance Amelia and Polly had attended. Holding up the Bible, he told them of his experiences in Mafeking, and of the young woman who had given him her own Bible when his had been lost in the cyclone. Her name? Captain Quarterman!

How proud Amelia and Polly were to hear of the work Daisy was doing, helping to care for the wounded in Mafeking's little hospital and providing food for the railway men suffering from the after effects of malaria. The sacrifice Amelia had made in allowing Daisy to go to South Africa had been well worthwhile.

Meanwhile, life was as busy as usual for Daisy and Lieutenant Cullinan, their meetings in the hall being always well attended. Not all the soldiers were well behaved, however, and it was on such occasions that another of Lieutenant Cullinan's talents—firmness—was invaluable. The Lieutenant had a way of handling men that commanded great respect from them, and Daisy was taking note of her tactics.

One evening one of the soldiers spoke to Daisy before the meeting.

"Captain," he said, "one of our men has taken on a bet that he'll go up to the Mercy Seat and ask to be saved tonight. I thought I had better warn you so that you can be prepared for him!"

"Thanks for the information. I'll be prepared all right," Daisy exclaimed, a glint in her eye.

When the hefty soldier blundered forward and knelt at the little altar rail, looking ever so penitent, Daisy leaned forward, grasped him by his collar and hauled him to his feet.

"Don't come here to make a mockery of religion," she said sternly, wagging an admonishing finger at him. "You don't want to be converted. Go back to your seat and collect your bet."

Laughter rippled round the hall as the mortified soldier beat a hasty retreat; but those seated in the front row could have sworn that a smile lurked around the lips of the stern face confronting them.

"I'm going to write to Walter tonight," Daisy told Lieutenant Cullinan on their walk home, "and I'll have lots to tell him," she chuckled, recalling the look of surprise on the soldier's face. "Normally I would never dream of doing such a drastic thing."

"But you did it. You made a statement about respect, and I don't think that young man will ever forget it," Lieutenant Cullinan replied with a grin.

Daisy and Walter corresponded regularly by mail, encouraging each other in their work and speculating when it would be possible for them to be married. Walter was still working among the troops and would remain there, possibly until the end of the war.

CHAPTER 17

THE WAR DRAGS ON

By July 1900, in the cold of the winter, many of the Boers had decided that it was futile to continue the war against the British. With heavy hearts they contemplated accepting Lord Roberts' offer to surrender their weapons and return to their farms. The relief of Ladysmith, Kimberley and Mafeking seemed to point to the rapidly approaching end of the war.

Then, to their surprise, the Boer leaders Christiaan de Wet and Jan Smuts, the brilliant young Boer general, began to succeed with their raids in the Orange Free State and the Cape Province. Revived in spirit, the Boers once again joined the Boer commandos in various parts of the country. This tragic, unfortunate war was to continue for a further eighteen months.

Although co-ordinated under the Boer General Louis Botha, these highly mobile commando units operated independently from their farms, to which they kept returning for supplies and food. They damaged railway lines more than a hundred times, attacked British forces, seized supplies and planned to invade the Cape. When the Boers destroyed the Pienaar's River bridge north of Pretoria, the frustrated British forces, numbering thousands of troops, hunted for De Wet. Their search was in vain.

Eventually, after some soul searching, the British introduced a 'scorched earth' policy to stop the Boers from carrying out attacks and retreating to their farms. This drastic step brought great anxiety and hardship to the Boer families. Houses were burned to the ground, cattle were driven away and crops were destroyed. All males were taken prisoner and women and children were taken away to British camps.

About thirty thousand farms and twenty small villages were eventually destroyed, first by Lord Roberts's and then by General Kitchener's scorched earth policies. Blackened, ruined buildings, flattened crops and an eerie silence over the land was all that remained of once fertile farms.

The camps housing the women and children, initially created as unofficial refugee camps, now became concentration camps under Kitchener. This had unforeseen, disastrous results, however, because thousands of women and children died of measles, dysentery, typhoid or malaria, as diseases spread rapidly through such large concentrations of people in relatively confined areas.

Boer prisoners captured by the British were deported to the island of St. Helena or to Ceylon, India or Bermuda. They remained there until the end of the war, when the Boers debated a peace proposal in the town of Vereeniging, and finally signed a Peace Treaty on May 31st, 1902 in Pretoria.

The bitterness felt by the Boers left a legacy for decades to come, which eventually was to shape the destiny of the divided country and have far reaching repercussions.

Daisy, mindful of the concern her family felt about her being in far away South Africa, wrote to her mother.

Dearest Mother, she wrote, *I am well and quite safe at present in Mafeking, and am getting on with my work, which is progressing. Please don't worry about me. Lieutenant Cullinan is a great help to me and we spend a great deal of time with the wounded soldiers and civilians at the hospital.*

Daisy had also turned her attention to the little cottage in which they were living. With a little ingenuity and a great deal of energy, their home was now more comfortable. Shelves had been fastened to the walls, the packing cases covered with bright curtaining and the window panes, damaged during the cyclone, had been replaced. A small coal stove, renovated and polished, now occupied the hearth and made cooking easier. Even the ants had been beaten and seldom intruded into the kitchen.

Two months had passed since the cyclone had struck the town. During that time the men had been hard at work, repairing the damaged buildings, little knowing that soon enough all their hard work would be wasted.

One bright, sunny afternoon Daisy was preparing for their daily visit to the hospital, when Lieutenant Cullinan glanced through the window.

"There's a huge, dark cloud in the sky!" she exclaimed, puzzled. Hurrying to the doorway she stopped suddenly and listened.

"Do you hear that sound coming towards us?" she asked.

"Yes," Daisy was equally puzzled, "it sounds like the sea."

"It's hail!" the Lieutenant announced. "Close the doors and windows—quickly!"

Seconds later their voices were drowned by the deafening sound of hailstones the size of golf balls pelting mercilessly down on the tin roof above them. The rain poured down, blocking everything from view, adding to the destruction being caused by the hail.

"Look, the roof"s leaking,"

Daisy cried, hurrying to the kitchen to look for a bucket.

"The hail's making holes in the roof!" exclaimed Lieutenant Cullinan. "We'll have to cut a hole in the ceiling to let the water out!"

Climbing onto the table, she slashed the calico ceiling with a bread knife. They were unprepared for the amount of water that poured down into the bucket, filling it to overflowing in a few seconds. New leaks appeared and they had no option but to resign themselves to a wet, uncomfortable afternoon.

Hastily donning coats, they put up their umbrellas for protection and perched on the bed, to await the end of the storm.

Despite their discomfort, Daisy couldn't help laughing.

"Can you imagine what our families would say if they could see us now—perched on the bed holding umbrellas over our heads?"

"They would probably be horrified!" Lieutenant Cullinan chuckled.

When at last the hail and rain stopped—almost as suddenly as it had started—the cottage was in a soggy mess. They set to work, sweeping the water through the doorway and mopping up the floor.

When they ventured outside the following morning they were amazed at the destruction caused by the hailstorm. Hardly a window pane remained in the houses; gardens and crops were flattened and trees were battered and stripped of their leaves and fruit.

The hardest hit section of the town was the village occupied by the cattle-keeping Baralong tribe. Cattle signified their wealth, and the loss of part of their herds was a severe blow to them.

Daisy and Lieutenant Cullinan went among the people, comforting them and offering practical help wherever possible. Seeing so much misery around them, they had no time to think of their own badly damaged home, with not one whole window pane left.

Daisy gazed with dismay at the battered, forlorn town and the dazed inhabitants wandering around amidst the destruction.

"Mafeking has indeed had more than it's share of trouble in the past year," she said sadly.

CHAPTER 18

DAISY AND WALTER ARE MARRIED

Six months had passed since Daisy had been sent back to Mafeking to re-establish the Corps on a sound footing. Six months in which she and Lieutenant Cullinan had had to face hardship and disappointment; but now, with the return of most of the townsfolk, the work was well established. Their task had been completed and it was time for them to move on, leaving behind with the Salvationists the memory of two spirited young women, standing on the street corners beneath the lamplight, their voices lifted in praise to the God they loved and served so diligently.

In January, 1901, Daisy found herself back in Kimberley, her task being to assist Staff-Captain Mayers with the growing evangelical work in the diamond fields. She was also nearer to Walter, who, after having been stationed in the Naval city of Simonstown, where he was engaged in working with the troops, had now been transferred to Grahamstown. Also, although the war was continuing in various parts of the country, it was relatively peaceful in the Eastern Cape. With his work with the troops completed, this meant that she and Walter could now go ahead with their plans to marry.

In June, 1901, Daisy packed her belongings and travelled from Kimberley to Cape Town where she stayed in the home of the Stevens family, to prepare for her wedding. During those few days she was also able to renew her friendship with Ethel, and the two young women had much to talk about.

"When I arrived in Cape Town from England I had no idea that I would be meeting my future husband," Daisy remarked, as Ethel helped her to get ready.

"As far as Walter is concerned, it was love at first sight! He couldn't take his eyes off you on that train journey to Queenstown," Ethel grinned.

Walter Scott and Daisy Quarterman,
on their wedding day, June 12th, 1901

The Citadel in Cape Town was packed on that sunny winter day of June 12th, 1901, for the marriage of Ensign Walter Scott and Captain Daisy Quarterman. Although dressed in a Salvation Army uniform, customary among their Officers, Daisy was as radiant as any bride in a traditional white dress. Walter, stealing a glance at her dimpled cheeks and shining blue eyes, was glad their long wait was over at last.

Staff-Captain Clack sang a solo of the special wedding song in the Salvation Army Songbook, "The Royal Marriage of the Lamb," followed by an address by Staff-Captain Mrs. Stevens, Daisy's "mother for the occasion."

"My friend, Amelia Quarterman, asked me to be a mother to her daughter when Daisy left Ealing four years ago, bound for South Africa," she said, "and it has been my great pleasure to do so. Daisy holds a special place in our hearts, and we are proud of her devotion and zeal for the Salvation Army cause."

"Not only do my husband and I regard her as our own daughter, but I feel that instead of losing a daughter, we have gained a son as well," she added, smiling with affection at Walter.

The Assistant Chief Secretary spoke of the sterling qualities of Ensign Scott, recalling how at one time the young man had been antagonistic towards the Army. Then he had become converted and was now a devoted worker.

The Commissioner urged them to trust God in every situation, and not be concerned about what would happen in the future. Then, as the young couple made their promises under the Blood and Fire Flag, Walter placed the ring on Daisy's finger and they were pronounced man and wife.

Being called upon to say a few words, the bridegroom expressed their determination to remain faithful to the cause so dear to their hearts, and to work with still greater energy to win souls for God.

After their wedding Daisy and Walter spent a few days in Cape Town before setting off by train to picturesque Grahamstown, where Walter was still stationed.

"Welcome to our new home!" beamed Walter, as he swept Daisy up in his arms and carried her over the threshold of the small cottage in the centre of the town. "We have to keep up with tradition, you know," he declared.

"It's special, because it is our first home," Daisy replied, as Walter put her down in the centre of the sparsely furnished sitting room. Mentally she noted how she could make it more comfortable. All it needed was a woman's touch, she decided, and their first home would be quite appealing.

The Corps welcomed Daisy with enthusiasm, for she was already well known for her work among young people; but their stay in Grahamstown was short lived, because two months later they were transferred to Port Elizabeth, again to do evangelical work among young people in the community.

When a year later, on June 2nd, 1902, they were blessed with a son, James (Jim), their happiness was complete. The Boer war had ended in May, so hopefully they would be able to consider visiting Daisy's family in England in a year's time, when Jim was old enough to travel.

How Daisy longed to see the dear, familiar faces of her family again. It was almost six years since that memorable day when she had set sail on the *Tintagel Castle*, leaving behind her beloved family as she journeyed to a land far away. During that time she had served in so many parts of South Africa, had many adventures and met and married the love of her life—Walter!

During the year that followed, Daisy revelled in being a young mother and having a child of her own. She could hardly wait to show him to her family in England. Salvation Army Officers were seldom stationed for long in any one town in those days, however, and they found themselves transferred again, this time to Kimberley.

Dear Polly and Nellie, she wrote to her sisters, *I can't wait to see you again and to show you our dear little son. I know that Mother will be glad to have another grandchild too. How I long to see James and his family as well.*

When Jim was a year old Daisy, Walter and Jim went to England on three months furlough. It was then 1903—seven years since Daisy had left for South Africa.

Standing on deck of the liner, watching the familiar coastline of the country of her birth loom into view, Daisy felt a surge of excitement.

"We'll be docking in Southampton soon, and setting off by train for London. Within a few hours I'll be seeing my dear family again!"

Amelia was overjoyed at their reunion. Now aged seventy-three and very frail, she had been persuaded to give up her home and was living with Polly in Lanark House, a Salvation Army home for the aged. Amelia's indomitable spirit was still evident, despite her frailty, and her faith in God was as strong as ever.

"Let me have a good look at you, Daisy," said Amelia, smiling as her gaze took in the slim young woman holding her lively one-year-old son in her arms, with Walter close beside her, "you're as pretty as ever. And what a lovely baby you have!"

Then turning to Walter, she held out her arms and said: "Walter, welcome to the family in England."

Their three months furlough flew by, with visits to Nellie, who was working for an elderly couple in Ealing, and to James and his wife Florence and sons Stanley, Bernard and Leonard, who were living in Great Yarmouth.

Then there was much to discuss with Polly, who was engaged in Rescue Staff work in England and Scotland, and was interested in the work Daisy and Walter had done in South Africa.

One morning there was a knock at the door, and upon opening it Daisy let out a joyful cry.

"Gertie! How wonderful to see you; and you have a lovely little girl too!"

The friends hugged each other, laughing as they went into the parlour.

"Walter, meet my dear friend Gertie. We spent many happy times together growing up."

"Were you there when Daisy pinned a carrot into the Sister's veil?" Walter enquired, a twinkle in his eye.

"Yes, I was," Gertie laughed, recalling the incident so many years before, and was eager to hear all the news of Daisy's adventures in South Africa.

"The last time I saw you," reflected Daisy, "was on the wharf, saying good-bye before I boarded the *Tintagel Castle*; and we were both crying."

"Well, I'm glad you're back—even if it is only for three months," Gertie replied.

There were many more friendships renewed, and Walter accompanied Daisy to visit her old Corps in Ealing, where they were enthusiastically welcomed. How interested her friends were to hear the tales they had to tell about their work in South Africa.

Looking at the mature, shining faced young woman bouncing her baby son on her knee, they found it hard to realize that she was the same rebel who had given her Captain grey hairs while she was growing up!

As the time drew near for her departure from England, Daisy was filled with sadness at the thought that she may never see her beloved mother again.

"Don't worry about Mother, Daisy. She is comfortable here and I will take good care of her, and see to her needs," Polly reassured her.

Standing on the deck of the ship taking them back to South Africa, Daisy waved a tearful farewell to her dear family gathered on the wharf below. She was leaving them once more, just as she had done seven years ago, she reflected, and she wondered when, if ever, she would see them again.

Slowly the ship pulled away from the wharf and the figures standing there became smaller and smaller as the liner put to sea. Walter slipped his arm around Daisy and she buried her face on his shoulder and sobbed.

Their visit to England had been opportune. A few months after their return to South Africa, Amelia, living in a Salvation Army home for the aged in St. Albans, fell ill with pneumonia and passed away on March 21st 1904, at the age of seventy-four years, with Polly beside her, holding her hand.

CHAPTER 19

THE STORM CLOUDS GATHER

Upon their arrival by ship in Cape Town Walter and Daisy reported to Headquarters, and were surprised to learn that Walter would soon be transferred to Cape Town. His task would be to work in a very poor area near the docks, called District Six, notorious for drunks and thugs. This would be very challenging work, but Walter prepared himself for the task.

"I'll help you by running the Sunday School, Walter," Daisy volunteered, "I have worked in that area before—and there are lots of other jobs I can do while Jim is asleep. We'll cope."

Returning to Kimberley, they packed their belongings, bade farewell to their fellow Salvationists and set off by train to Cape Town, the city they both loved so much and which held so many happy memories for them.

On January 22nd 1904, their daughter was born in Cape Town, and in keeping with the custom of that time, the baby was named Daisy after her mother.

After working for several months among the people in District Six, Walter was placed in charge of the Subscribers' Department at the Cape Town Headquarters, and part of his responsibilities was to make frequent trips into the countryside on his bicycle to collect funds.

Watching him pack his rucksack Daisy's heart would cry: "Don't go again so soon, dear; the children and I need you so much." But her thoughts went unuttered—for he was setting out to do God's work—and she had no wish to hold him back, no matter how great her need of him.

Instead she would smile and place a few more biscuits in his lunch tin, and hope that his rolled up blanket, strapped behind the saddle of his bicycle, would keep him warm. Should he not be offered a warm bed at some farmer's home, he would be forced to spend the night in the bush.

While he was away the time went by quickly enough, for Daisy was kept busy looking after the children. Also, as every Salvation Army Officer is a friend to the needy, hardly a day went by without a knock at the door by someone needing a word of encouragement or a helping hand.

Respecting Amelia's last wish, Polly asked to be transferred to Cape Town to be near Daisy, and in 1904 she arrived in Cape Town to take up the appointment of Matron in the Salvation Army's Rescue Home. Daisy was delighted to see her gentle, caring sister again, and to know that she would be near her and her small children.

On March 21st, 1905, their second son, Percy, was born, and when he was four years old their third son, Walter (Wally) was born on May 16th, 1909, and was named after his father. Daisy was kept busy, caring for the children and helping Walter with his work wherever she could.

When Wally was only a month old the young couple were dealt a severe blow. Walter, who had been pale and listless for several months and had a continuous cough, consulted a doctor. Seeing him walking up the path, Daisy went to the door to meet him.

"What did the doctor say, dear?" she enquired.

"I thought it was only a cold, Daisy," Walter replied slowly, hanging up his coat as he spoke, "but it was more serious than that."

"What did he find, Walter?" Daisy asked uneasily.

"I have tuberculosis—and you know it's an almost incurable disease," he replied.

Daisy sat down unsteadily on a chair. Tuberculosis! Her beloved Walter; so young and afflicted by a dreaded disease! What could they do about it?

When Walter's doctor advised him to move immediately to a drier climate, Headquarters decided to send them on transfer away from the coast, to Bloemfontein, a city in the Orange Free State.

Daisy heard the news with a sense of relief.

"The patch on my lung was healed when I moved to a drier climate. I'm sure you will benefit from a drier climate too, Walter," she suggested hopefully.

By the time they moved it was July, in the middle of winter, and Bloemfontein greeted them with a freezing cold wind. Then as the summer approached it became unbearably hot.

Walter's mother, Anne Scott, then eighty-four years old and still sprightly, went to live with them and lightened Daisy's burden considerably. Accustomed to hard work all her life, she would rise at four o'clock in the morning and have a cold bath, then proceed to bake the daily bread, which she served hot at the breakfast table.

Walter's health was gradually declining, and Daisy spent more of her time with him, while Walter's mother cared for the children. Having to spend so much time in bed he found the heat unbearable, and was most relieved and grateful when his brother George, who owned a sheep farm in Barclay East, invited the family to spend a few months there.

Full of high hope Daisy packed the family's belongings and they set off shortly before Christmas, travelling part of the way—from the town of Lady Grey to Barclay East—by ox wagon.

"Walter, you'll be able to rest and have plenty of fresh air and healthy, homegrown food, and you'll begin to regain your health," said Daisy.

"I hope so," was Walter's reply, "because I'm looking forward to resuming my duties."

Propped up on a couch on the wide verandah of the old farm house, Walter spent most of his time revelling in the beautiful mountain scenery and writing letters of encouragement and inspiration to friends and acquaintances alike.

The children were delighted with farm life. Milk, fruit and vegetables were plentiful—and so were Uncle George's fifteen cats, which would sit under the massive dining-room table waiting for treats. George didn't have the heart to drown a cat. As they multiplied he would take a drive into the countryside with a basket full of cats and let them loose on each farmer's property, knowing the farmer would take pity on them and allow them to stay.

Jim's school lessons continued uninterrupted, for George and Esther had a governess to teach their seven children. Life was leisurely and peaceful, providing Daisy with a well-needed rest.

Even baby Wally was contented, and when his two glass bottles eventually broke, Esther took him into the dairy, dipped a ladle into a bucket of milk, and gave it to him to drink. He soon grew into a healthy, bonny baby.

Daisy was not to know that the four happy months spent on the farm were the lull before the storm. Walter's health declined still further, despite the healthy country air, and it was decided that they should return to Bloemfontein. The doctor put Walter into the National Hospital.

One day blurred into the next, with Daisy making daily visits to the hospital, while Walter's mother looked after the children. One young woman whose husband was dying of tuberculosis spent a great deal of time in the hospital as well.

"Thank goodness I have no children," she remarked to Daisy one day, "I pity you having to bring up your four young children on your own."

For a moment Daisy was tempted to reply with spirit, but after a glance at the woman's drawn, discouraged face she felt nothing but compassion. When this woman's husband was gone, she would have nothing left in life.

"Well, I don't regret having had them," she replied softly, "They are part of my husband and I will have them for comfort."

The days stretched into months, with Walter's decline becoming even more alarming. His once healthy body became painfully thin and racked with coughing; yet through it all his will to survive shone through like a ray of sunshine, his faith in God never wavering.

In a letter to *The War Cry* on 17th November, 1910, he wrote:

> *I would not have been without this experience that God, in His love and wisdom, has permitted me to pass through, for worlds. I shall ever praise Him for it. With the Psalmist I can now say: 'It is good for me that I have been afflicted.*

Despite his weakness, Walter was spurred on during the last few weeks of his life to write to friends and fellow Officers all over the country, which must have expended much of his energy.

Those were dark days for Daisy, who scarcely left his bedside. Realizing the shadows were gathering even deeper around them, they faced the future together, weeping at the thought of parting, and praying together for the strength to face whatever God had planned for them.

"Daisy, your bright, cheerful spirit has given me courage and strength during these past months," Walter told her in their last few days together. "I would like to live for your sake, dearest, and for the sake of our precious children; but I'm fully resigned to God's will, whichever way it is. For whether we live, we live unto the Lord; whether we die, we die unto the Lord. Living or dying, we are the Lord's."

As Daisy sat beside Walter through his last few hours and watched him slipping peacefully away from this life, she felt that for him death had no sting. Almost his last words to her before she kissed him goodbye were: "Don't you hear the band playing, dear; can't you hear them?" Then he murmured softly: "Jesus is a rock in a weary land, a shelter in the time of storm." And then he was gone. She was alone.

Alone at Walter's bedside, with the early morning sun streaming down onto her tear-stained face, her hands clasped tightly in prayer. It was 6.40 a.m. on that Wednesday morning of November 30th 1910, and Walter was only forty years old.

She did not know how long she sat there, wearily unable to move. At last she arose and stumbled from the room and someone took her home. How, she wondered, would she be able to break the news to her anxious family?

Old Mrs. Scott had no need for words. The weary stoop of her daughter-in-law's shoulders and her drawn face told her the news at once. Taking her hand she led Daisy into the bedroom, where both women wept for the man they had loved so much. Then, kneeling side by side, they prayed for Walter's soul, praising God for making it possible for him to do so much good during his lifetime.

When Daisy rose to her feet she was confronted by eight-year-old Jim and six-year-old Daisy, their enquiring faces turned to her.

"Daddy has gone to Heaven to live with Jesus," she said as calmly as she was able, and comforted them as their tears flowed.

"And now, Jim," Daisy said later, "you can help me by being the man about the house!"

"I don't want to go to school today, Mom," Jim said slowly. "I'd rather stay at home with you. You'll need me to look after you."

"Yes, of course," agreed Daisy, "and you could be of great help to me."

Walter's funeral service was attended by many Salvation Army officers, among them being Lieut. Colonel Van Rossum, Brigadier King, Adjutant Hardy, Adjutant Pierce and Adjutant Miller, who paid tribute to their comrade for his strong character and zeal in his work.

Daisy, standing with her mother-in-law and children, paid tribute to her husband.

"This is the saddest day of my life," said Daisy, "yet I do not look only at the grave, but beyond, and am determined to carry on his work," she said. "It has been hard for me to see my dear husband suffer, but I know that he is now safe and will suffer no longer. I realize that the hardest part is yet to come, so I will go one step at a time, trusting in Him who has never yet failed me."

After Lieutenant Colonel Van Rossum had read the burial portion of Scripture, Daisy's three elder children each placed on the coffin a tiny bunch of flowers. As the last strains of "Rock of Ages" died away, Walter was laid to rest.

Anne Scott

CHAPTER 20

ANOTHER DOOR OPENS

Eighteen months of strain had taken their toll on Daisy. Mentally and physically exhausted, she decided to send Jim to Walter's sister in Lady Frere for a holiday, while she went with the other children and Granny Scott to her sister-in-law and brother-in-law, Colonel and Mrs. Rauch, in Cape Town.

Gradually as the weeks went by her strength returned, and although her heart ached with the emptiness of life without Walter, she learned to cope with her sorrow. In the meantime, Jim began attending school in Lady Frere with his cousins, and young Daisy was enrolled at the local school in Cape Town.

"The time has come for me to consider the future of my children and myself," she declared to Granny Scott. With no husband to support them it would be difficult to bring up four children on her own. "I think that for the time being," she added reluctantly, "Jim and Daisy will benefit most by being left in the schools they have just started. I'll keep Percy and Wally with me."

Earnestly she prayed to God for guidance, trusting He would open up the way forward.

Meanwhile Polly, now Adjutant Quarterman, had been transferred from Cape Town to Kimberley to run the Salvation Army's unmarried mothers' home. Polly needed a helper, and who would be a better helper than Daisy?

Just as one door had closed, another had opened, and Daisy found herself back in Kimberley, where her two little sons soon settled down happily to life in the home.

This field of service was new to Daisy, but her years of training in the Salvation Army had taught her adaptability. It was also good for her to be working with her sister, who would be able to help provide a stable atmosphere for the two young boys.

Daisy soon found that the young girls needed not only moral support, but practical help as well, for many of them had come from poor homes. With her usual enthusiasm for tackling any job, she was soon teaching them needlework, which she sold for them.

Having worked with young people in the past, Daisy felt empathy and compassion for these lonely, frightened young girls, whose parents had sent them away to have their babies. Adoption agencies usually arranged to have their babies placed with childless couples, who would bring up the child as their own. Many a young mother wept on Daisy's shoulder at the sight of their baby being taken away.

Eighteen months later, in 1912, Daisy was once again transferred, this time to Johannesburg, the booming "City of Gold," as it was known to miners from around the world. Her task was to do evangelical work among the Cornish miners in the suburb of Fordsburg.

It was a bitterly cold day when the train arrived in Johannesburg. Captain van der Watt, who was to be her assistant, waited at the station to meet the young mother who alighted from the train, clutching each of her small sons by the hand. Soon the kindly Captain had the tired trio seated beside a cosy fire in the sitting room while she prepared supper in the kitchen.

Seated around the kitchen table with a steaming bowl of soup before them, Daisy looked around the room with interest, as this was to be their new home. The water in the kettle boiled while the Captain arranged the teacups and scooped two large teaspoons of Mazawattee tea out of the brightly coloured tin bearing a picture of a grandmother and her granddaughter drinking tea. She tossed the tea leaves into the teapot and covered it carefully with a knitted tea cosy, then placed it on the side of the wood-fired stove to keep warm while it steeped. She then cut thick slices of home-made bread, still warm from the oven, which she placed on the table.

In the corner of the room stood a zinc-lined oak ice-chest for which 'crystal ice' would be delivered weekly, to keep food fresh and cool. From the ceiling nearby dangled a fly paper, curled and saturated with golden syrup and melted resin to trap any errant flies, and on a shelf in the kitchen stood a small, blue metal medicine box. Curtains made of red and white checked gingham material framed the window above the kitchen sink, and resting in a soap holder on the sink was a bar of soap made from rendered down fat and lye.

"We hold most of our meetings in a little wood and iron building," Captain van der Watt informed her, "and it's always packed with miners, most of them Cornish. They are a long way from home and sometimes get very lonely. They earn plenty of money on the mines, and are very generous to us."

"I'm looking forward to this new type of work," commented Daisy, scooping up the last spoonful of tasty soup and spreading some home-made apricot jam on the left-over piece of bread on her plate.

After supper Daisy took the two little boys to the bathroom where hot water from the wood-fired copper boiler spurted out of the tap into the cast iron bath with its claw feet. After bathing them she put their pajamas, dressing gowns and slippers on them, then passed them to the Captain while she used the same bath water for her own bath. Water was used sparingly, due to the drought affecting many parts of South Africa.

As the months went by Captain van der Watt proved to be a great help to Daisy, often caring for the children while she was busy with her work. But much work was to be done by both of them—visiting, conducting services and selling *The War Cry*—and at times Daisy returned home worn out from the effort.

One afternoon, when Captain van der Watt had been called out and young Percy had been left alone to care for his little brother Wally, Daisy returned home to find Percy sitting on the doorstep, smiling happily. He had neatly set the table in the kitchen, put the kettle on the stove to boil and placed her slippers beside her easy chair.

"How thankful I am to have such a thoughtful son!" she exclaimed, giving Percy a hug. Daisy may not have realized it, but she possessed that rare ability to bring out the best in everyone.

The early part of the 20th century had brought about many changes in everyday life. In 1900 the Eastman Kodak Company began producing its "Brownie" camera for the mass market, in 1901 an American named King Camp Gillette invented razor blades and in Scotland Yard in London identifying people by means of fingerprinting was introduced. Marconi successfully transmitted the first wireless radio signal across the Atlantic Ocean in 1901 and in December 1903 the brothers Orwell and Wilbur Wright triumphantly completed the first controlled flight in a powered aircraft named the *Kitty Hawk* in North Carolina. Thomas Edison had invented the first electric light bulb in 1879, but electricity was not generally used in many homes in the early 1900s. Even telephones, although invented in 1876 by Alexander Graham Bell, were still not widely used due to their expense, and business correspondence was hand written by clerks and secretaries and delivered by mail. Typewriters, invented in the 1870's, were still being developed and improved, and were not generally in use until after 1900.

However, rapid progress was being made in all areas of life, thus improving living conditions generally. Electricity began to replace steam power for driving machinery, the automobile industry grew rapidly and the Model T Ford car was mass—produced in the United States. In July 1907 Colonel Robert Baden-Powell, inspired by the scouts used by the army in Mafeking during the Boer War, formed the

Boy Scouts movement to encourage discipline and a sense of duty. In 1909 French aviator Louis Bleriot flew across the English Channel in a wooden monoplane.

Then, in 1912, the impressive new ship *Titanic*, thought to be unsinkable, hit an iceberg off the coast of Canada and sank. Only 705 of the 2,227 passengers survived in the frigid weather.

Meanwhile, in South Africa, Lord Milner became the Governor of the Transvaal and the Orange River Colony following the defeat of the Boers in the Boer War. Over the years he concentrated on rebuilding the country and brought in a team of experts from Britain who built new roads and railways and introduced farming projects and new forestry schemes. They were hampered in their work, to a certain extent, by a severe drought that lasted from 1903 to 1908, in which many streams and even rivers dried up.

Friction between the English and the Dutch settlers still existed, with Lord Milner insisting that English be the only official language and the Boers demanding that Dutch have equal status. Gradually over the years the Dutch (Boers) became known as the Afrikaners, and the language they spoke, which had evolved from Dutch, became known as Afrikaans. Eventually the two sides became more conciliatory towards each other in an effort to unite the country.

On May 31st, 1910, the Union of South Africa came into being, amidst celebrations throughout the country and a pageant in Cape Town with fireworks displays and concerts. The Duke and Duchess of Connaught, who had arrived from Britain on the *Balmoral Castle*, represented the King of England and opened the first Union Parliament.

One of the exciting events of 1910 was witnessing Halley's Comet. The *Cape Argus* newspaper declared that although the earth would pass through the comet's tail, particles could not penetrate the surface of the earth because the earth was 'covered with a shell of atmosphere very much denser than the comet's tail.'

So much was happening world wide, politically and socially as well as scientifically, that people found it quite bewildering at times.

Entertainment was usually in the form of musical evenings in the home, with the mother playing the piano and the family gathered around singing such songs as *Clementine* and *Campdown Races*. They also sang Christmas carols and hymns. The pianola was popular because it could be played by people who had never learned music. It was loaded with perforated rollers that carried the music, while the player laboriously pumped the bellows to blow it strongly enough to produce the music.

Most popular with the children was the Magic Lantern, bought with a selection of slides with prices starting at three shillings and eleven pence. The images were projected through lenses onto a screen, with the aid of paraffin lamps as a source of light.

Saturday was always an exciting day in most towns, with the farmers coming into town in their ox wagons, Cape carts and buggies, to sell their wares and stock up on the supplies they needed. The women stood around in small groups in the street, sharing news of their families and discreetly surveying each other's dresses and hats, while the tinkle of bells attracted the excited children to the ice cream carts.

Annual church bazaars and the local agricultural show featured strongly in every community, with stalls laden with jars of fruit, vegetables, cakes and milk tarts. They were famous for their "koeksusters," twisted strips of fried dough saturated in golden syrup, and "boerewors," (farmer's sausage rich in spices.) The women took great pride in their produce.

Sunday afternoons were usually spent visiting a park. Those fortunate enough to live near the Johannesburg Zoo would make their way to the ornate bandstand to listen to the music. Members of the Returned Soldiers, in serge uniforms and wearing white peak caps, along with the Salvation Army band, military brass bands and school bands, took turns in entertaining the crowd spread out over the lawn on picnic rugs.

The boys, dressed in sailor suits or woollen knickerbockers and boots, and the girls in silk dresses tied with sashes and wide-brimmed hats and gloves, waited in turn for the highlight of their day—a ride on one of the elephants! The elephants had saddles on their backs to which a row of wooden seats were firmly fastened on either side. Four children sat on each side, securely fastened in. The trainer signalled the bandmaster when the elephants were ready, the band began to play and the elephants ambled off on their journey around the park.

Despite the heat, the men always wore ties and the women wore long dresses and starched petticoats, with large hats and parasols for protection from the hot sun.

Another event was the circus, which travelled from town to town and attracted huge crowds, eager to see the animals, trapeze artists and clowns. Fairs were also very popular, with the Ferris Wheel being a draw card, while the children enjoyed the '*Merry go Round*' or roundabout and the numerous stalls.

Motor cars were becoming much more common and with them the demand for improvement of the roads, many of which were little more than cart tracks in the countryside. Over time, and under the direction of the engineers and road experts brought in from Britain, the roads improved. Horse drawn carts were still in use but motor vehicles were slowly replacing them.

And so life proceeded at a fairly leisurely pace, until 1914, when the first turbulent political rumbles of an imminent war began to surface. The First World War was triggered by the action of one man—a Serbian nationalist named Gavril Princip, who assassinated the heir to the Austro-Hungarian throne, Archduke Franz Ferdinand, and his wife on June 28th, 1914. The Austrians declared war on Serbia, and within months this regional conflict quickly escalated into a war involving all the major European powers, with Germany and the Austro-Hungarians in conflict with Britain, France and Russia. The First World War (then referred to as the Great War) had begun and was to last four years, causing massive destruction and the loss of millions of lives.

South Africans, rallying to the call, declared war on September 8th, 1914, despite divided loyalties and resentment still felt by many Afrikaners following the Boer War. At Britain's request, South Africa invaded German South West Africa and East Africa to secure the areas. Troops were also sent to Belgium and Northern France, where they took part in the great Somme offensive on the Western Front in July, 1916. Many of them fought and died in the muddy trenches and open plains of Flanders' fields in Belgium and in a wood, called Delville Wood, near the French village of Longueval.

Feelings ran high in the city of Johannesburg. Many Germans, who had become South African citizens, suddenly found their businesses being burned down, and most of them were interned for the duration of the war.

Appalled by the senselessness and cruelty of war, Daisy and her fellow Salvation Army Officers were kept busy comforting and helping the women whose husbands had left to fight in countries thousands of miles away. There were tearful scenes at railway stations across the country as families bade farewell to troops boarding trains bound for the troop ships in Cape Town. Some of the most poignant songs rendered at these partings were the popular "*Goodbye, Dolly Gray,*" and the well loved "*Tipperary.*"

Daisy and her children looked forward to the school holidays, when young Daisy and Jim travelled home, to be joyfully reunited with their family. How Daisy longed to be in a position to have her two older children living with her, but for the time being this was impossible. She could not support four children adequately on the salary she earned, and as the children grew older and their clothing became more expensive, she was often hard pressed to find enough money to go around. Yet somehow, just when she felt most desperate, something would turn up to ease her financial burden.

One cold winter day, when the children were pointing out the holes in their shoes, there was a knock at the door. It was the postman, with a registered letter. Intrigued, she tore it open and was amazed to find, folded within the letter, two ten pound notes!

"Some time ago," the writer explained, "when your husband was in business with his brother-in-law, Mr. Garrett, I owed them twenty pounds. When I was unable to pay it, your husband wrote it off as a bad debt, but it has been on my conscience ever since. Now I am in a position to repay that debt and therefore enclose the amount, in the hope that you will find it of use."

"Find it of use!" Daisy echoed jubilantly, "Now you shall all have a new pair of shoes and there will still be some left. This money will solve all our immediate problems." Her prayers had been answered in a most unexpected way.

Jim. Percy, Wally, Daisy and Daisy Jr. 1914.

Once again Daisy was transferred, this time to the town of Kroonstad, a quiet little town with a lovely river. It was now 1915, and South Africa had been in the grip of yet another severe drought. So severe, in fact, that the river bed of the Vaal River in Kroonstad had been completely dry for several months.

The farmers in the area lost many of their cattle and sheep due to the lack of water, and their normally fertile fields held forlorn stalks of dried out corn. The situation continued for some time and was becoming one of the worst droughts in the history of South Africa. Then suddenly, the rains came, the drought broke and the Vaal River changed overnight into a raging torrent.

Daisy worked mainly among the people who lived in the railway camp, and life was quiet and uneventful, providing her with an opportunity to have a little more rest.

In Europe, however, the war raged on, claiming millions of lives. Women in South Africa knitted socks, balaclavas and scarves for their soldiers, held bazaars and patriotic concerts to raise funds for the war effort and went to work in factories. They drove buses and ambulances (until now jobs held by men), and joined the Police Force, to replace the men who had left for war.

Women's dresses became less full, softer and shorter, due to the shortage of material. Flannel, cotton and taffeta became more popular, and women discarded their large hats in favour of smaller, more sensible ones, some of which were modelled on the hats worn by the Canadian Mounties! Even shoes were redesigned with cloth tops, as all available leather was used to manufacture boots for the soldiers.

Due to the shortage of imported goods, South Africans became more self-reliant and produced more food and commodities, and as a result English and Afrikaans citizens realized that they needed to work together for the common good of the country.

CHAPTER 21

THE FLU EPIDEMIC STRIKES

In January, 1917, Daisy was transferred yet again, to Pietermaritzburg to take charge of the local Corps in Chapel Street. How pleasant it was to be living in this beautiful, hilly city with its stately old buildings and spreading jacaranda trees. The gardens were a riot of colour, with purple and pink bougainvillia cascading over walls and azalea shrubs, covered in large pink blossoms, growing in profusion in parks and on the hillsides. Daisy took to this rambling old city at once.

"I know we are going to be very happy here," she enthused, and she was right, for not long afterwards she was able to send for Jim and her daughter Daisy to return home after they had lived with relatives for several years, and the family was once more reunited. Jim was now fifteen years old and Daisy was thirteen. Then, to add to her joy, her sister Polly, now sixty-two years old, was sent to help her with the evangelical work.

There was much to be done in the city, for the Salvation Army had a fairly large following, and Daisy was kept busy with her work and in caring for her family. Over the years she had taught her children to be self-sufficient, and this training was now coming in useful. While out on her rounds she knew that her children were capable of taking care of themselves, and on Sunday mornings each child willingly helped prepare the hall for the service.

September heralded the arrival of the mauve jacaranda blossoms, covering the trees all over the city and carpeting the hillsides with their delicate blooms. Daisy and her family climbed a hill to drink in the beauty of the soft blanket of mauve caressing the city in the spring sunshine.

On September 14th, 1918, a serious epidemic of Spanish influenza broke out in Durban and other South African ports and spread rapidly to Johannesburg and surrounding areas, afflicting eighteen thousand people in one month. Durban reported two thousand cases in four weeks. The total population of the country was reported as six million, and of these over two million contracted the disease, leading to the deaths of nearly a hundred and forty thousand people. Schools, shops and factories closed their doors, trains and trams ran less often and food became scarce. Hospitals were overflowing, doctors and nurses were collapsing with overwork and undertakers could not keep up with the demand for coffins. Mass graves were dug to bury the dead.

The epidemic was so serious that it was likened to the Bubonic Plague that had raged in London centuries before. In many cases whole families were confined to bed, unable to help each other.

Scorning the popular belief that sucking garlic would stave off the flu, Daisy made little muslin bags which she filled with camphor. Her family wore these around their necks, and fortunately none of them became ill.

Relief work among the city's large population was desperately needed, therefore Daisy wrote to the *Natal Witness* newspaper, asking the public for donations of meat for making soup at the Salvation Army's Home for Men. This would be distributed to those who were too ill to care for themselves.

The response was instant and encouraging. As well as meat donations from some firms, one store donated a large supply of billy cans in which to carry the soup. Others donated jellies and milk, farmers donated eggs and lemons, while Hayes Biscuit Factory supplied a generous amount of broken biscuits. These were put into packets ready for distribution with the soup.

The Boy Scouts Troop to which Percy belonged made frequent trips with carts to neighbouring farms to collect fruit, and helped with the distribution of soup and baked custard to the sick.

Working from early morning until late at night, Daisy and Polly arranged for a small band of women to help prepare and deliver the food. Polly and her friends, laden with baskets of foods, travelled by rickshaws (carts pulled by men), but Daisy, disliking the jerky movement of the rickshaws, preferred to walk.

While the epidemic was at its height the Mayor, Councillor A.E. Harwin, cancelled all church services and public gatherings, and took an interest in the relief work which Daisy and Polly had organized. He donated twenty-five pounds towards it himself, then accompanied Daisy on her rounds, to find out first hand how the people of his city were faring.

One of the stricken, who by then had become acquainted with Daisy, looked up at the Mayor and enquired: "Is this your husband, Captain?" and while she coloured with embarrassment the Mayor smiled and replied: "No, just a friend."

After six weeks the epidemic abated almost as suddenly as it had started, and a church service was held in the grounds of St. Peter's Church. The Salvation Army, its band of helpers and Daisy and Polly in particular were thanked for their unstinting efforts in the city's time of need.

On the 11th hour of November 11th, 1918, armistice was declared and the First World War came to an end. The City Hall was outlined with coloured lights and the residents of Pietermaritzburg celebrated in the streets, dancing and singing, in thankfulness that the "war to end all wars" had at last come to an end.

Christmas festivities were the happiest they had been for the past four years, but for many families there was an empty place at the table that would never again be filled.

In January 1919 Daisy was persuaded to take a short holiday at the coast, accompanied by her children, to recuperate after her hard work during the past three months.

In a written report, accompanied by photographs in the *Natal Witness,* Daisy was mentioned as having become well known for her work during the flu epidemic. She and Polly (Staff-Captain Mary Quarterman) were congratulated on having received their Long Service Badges from the Salvation Army in recognition of their having completed twenty-five years of unbroken service in South Africa.

From the time that Polly had received her first commission in London in 1886, she had worked tirelessly for the Salvation Army and had never married.

"Indeed!" she remarked indignantly, "I have had enough work to keep me occupied; there has been no time to even *think* of marriage!-

On January 12th, 1921, Daisy and Polly received word that ninety-two year old Granny Scott had passed away, after an illness lasting six months, leaving behind a large family who had loved her dearly. She had borne 14 children and had 65 grandchildren and 50 great grandchildren.

Daisy paid a fitting tribute to her, which was printed in *The War Cry.*

Proud to Wear its Uniform.

"Granny passed away at midnight." Thus ran the telegram I received on Wednesday morning. Though not altogether unexpected, knowing that for months dear Granny had been gradually growing weaker, yet the news came as a shock. It was hard to realize that after months of suffering, patiently borne, she had gone into the presence of her Lord, whom she loved and served faithfully for so many years.

Mother was a real out-and-out Salvationist. She loved the Army. Though not one of those who did public work, yet it was a joy for her to attend the Meetings, and she sought to cheer all those who came in touch with her.

For over four years Mother lived in our home and blessed us with her presence, and helped us with her counsel and advice.

She was a great lover of children, especially the tiny ones. How well they knew Granny's voice, and how lovingly she nursed and cared for them, that the mother might go out on the Master's business.

In sorrow and bereavement she was a wonderful example of fortitude, and always manifested an unwavering faith in God.

Sweet and hallowed memories will live on in the hearts of her children and grandchildren, and all who knew and loved her.

Oh, that each day of His coming may say:
"I have fought my way through;
I have finished the work Thou didst give me to do."

Staff-Captain Mrs. D.R. Scott.

CHAPTER 22

A NEW FIELD OF SERVICE

After three happy years in Pietermaritzburg, during which time Jim, now a young man, had started work on the Railways, Daisy learned with dismay that she was again being transferred, this time to Pretoria. This would mean parting once more from her eldest son, who was doing an apprenticeship with the Railways and would have to remain in Pietermaritzburg until its completion.

How difficult it was at times to perform her duties as an Army Officer and still see to the needs of her family. Yet instinctively she felt that if God had work for her to do elsewhere, she should go without hesitation.

In this frame of mind she attended a large farewell social, which the Corps had arranged for her, and at which the Mayor, among others, paid tribute to her outstanding service to the community.

The Scott family packed up and moved to Pretoria in the Transvaal, where Daisy took command of the Pretoria Corps. Her daughter Daisy, now a young woman, went to work at the Geological Survey Department in Pretoria, where she met and later married Francis Partridge, a well-respected mineralogist.

In 1923 Daisy was transferred yet again—this time being given a completely new field of service. The Salvation Army had bought the old Simmer and Jack Mine Hospital at the Driehoek Mine near the town of Germiston, with the intention of converting it into a Home for Girls. They needed a Matron and felt that Daisy would be the ideal person to run it, with Polly, now aged sixty-seven years, as her assistant.

Polly and Daisy inspected the old building, noting that it had been solidly built.

"A little bit of painting and renovating is all it needs," commented Daisy, "and it could be made into a comfortable home for the girls."

"And it has a big garden—with lots of weeds!" laughed Polly.

"Never mind. We'll soon sort it all out, and besides, we even have a few fruit trees. Look at this lovely old chestnut tree. We could put a bench under it and it would be a shady place to sit on a hot day."

When renovations to the rambling old building were completed and the garden tidied, the doors of the home were opened to the first six girls. Four of them were brought by their grandfather, the eldest child being eight years old and the youngest three.

"Their father is dead," he explained, very distressed, "and my grandchildren have been living in a tent with their mother. Now she has deserted them!"

Daisy welcomed the girls with her warm smile and showed them to their bedroom, and from then onwards she was their "new mother" to whom they came each night for their good-night kiss.

Another child had rickets and had to be nursed back to health, while yet another, a little redhead who had had a rough upbringing, told with relish the story of how her angry mother had thrown a pot of stew over her father when he returned home drunk.

One little seven-year-old, whose stepmother had frequently beaten her with a belt and dragged her around by her hair, was brought to the Home. Filled with compassion, Daisy held out her arms in a welcoming gesture. For one long moment the little girl surveyed Daisy, then her thin little face broke into a smile and she exclaimed: "At last—I've found a *real* mother!"

A staunch believer in routine and discipline, especially where young people were concerned, Daisy worked out a time-table to which each child adhered. The girls arose at 6 a.m., washed, dressed, made their beds and swept the dormitories. She always tried to make work a pleasure, and as they all worked they sang Salvation Army songs and choruses.

At seven o'clock breakfast was served, followed by prayers, after which the girls set off for school. At night, after evening prayers, she always had a personal chat with each of the girls before they went to bed.

As more girls were brought to the Home, the older girls were given lessons in typing and sewing, while Polly spent much of her time teaching them to knit by hand and to use a knitting machine.

Not only did the girls find a friend in need in Daisy, but even the local tramps did as well. They would arrive each day and sit on the bench under the huge chestnut tree in the garden, waiting for the bowl of hot, nourishing soup and bread that she never failed to provide for them.

"One can't reach a man's soul if his stomach is empty," was her practical remark as she busied herself in the kitchen.

Less than two and a half years after the inauguration of the Driehoek Home for Girls, Daisy's young charges had increased to sixty-five in number, their ages ranging from three to sixteen years.

By this time Daisy, always a lover of band music, had formed a mandolin band, with Adjutant Thomas Bentley as their trainer. Forty enthusiastic girls took part, rendering with precision their items of music and songs, drills and displays.

One evening the girls performed at the Johannesburg 1 Corps hall to a large and appreciative audience.

"The selection of the items by the mandolin band and their excellent rendition, reveals the interest taken in the girls and how the Home provides for their general development," said Major Carter, presiding over the gathering. "The girls show great keenness, and their deportment and work reflect credit on them, the Matron and Adjutant Bentley," he added.

Then, to their surprise, Commandant le Roux, on behalf of the Johannesburg Corps, presented Daisy with a "cello."

"Please accept this, Staff-Captain Scott, towards the Home Orchestra you're planning," he smiled, and to their even greater surprise, representatives of the various Corps of the Northern Division presented instruments to the girls.

The girls of the mandolin band had expressed a desire to form an orchestra, but had been hampered by the cost. Now the instruments given would enable them to go ahead with their plans. Daisy, Polly and the girls were overwhelmed by this kindness, and returned home with glad hearts, and with plans for still greater achievements in the future.

Working with the girls in her care, Daisy's aim was to be a mother in every way. Writing of them to *The War Cry*, she said:

> *When one of them comes to me and says: 'Matron, may I see you by yourself when you have time?' quite frequently there is some wrong to be confessed or some spiritual difficulty for which they need advice. I have spent many a profitable hour with these dear girls, some of whom have wept on my shoulder, and we have knelt together in prayer. The child has gone away with fresh courage and strength to fight the bad habit.*
> *One night, when all the others were in bed, and I thought asleep, I heard a voice singing. Looking through the dormitory window I saw a little girl of eleven years of age kneeling at her bedside and singing these words:*
> *'Trust and obey, for there's no other way,*
> *To be happy in Jesus, but to trust and obey.'*

Then she prayed: "O Lord Jesus, help me to trust and obey. Help me when I leave this good Home to be just as good outside as I am in here. Help my father and my mother, and bless Matron and all the children, for Jesus' sake, Amen."

She went home shortly afterwards, and when the father came to fetch her I told him the story. I said to him: 'You must help her.' His eyes filled with tears, and he said: 'I will, by God's grace.' He had recently been converted himself and was now trying to improve his life and make a decent home for his wife and children

Christmas was a particularly happy time at the Home. The girls made paper decorations for the Christmas tree, made small gifts for each other or bought something small with their carefully saved pocket money. One Christmas little Patti had no money and no gift for Daisy. Nothing she could make would be good enough for the Matron, she thought. At last, after days of puzzling over what to do, she solved her problem. Creeping stealthily to Daisy's door, she slipped under it a note in an envelope.

Picking it up in surprise, Daisy recognized Patti's childish handwriting at once.

"Dear Matron," Daisy read, her face softening, "I have no present to give you, and no money to buy one, but I will give you my obedience and love."

"Patti," whispered Daisy when she saw the little girl that evening, "your present was the best one of all!" The child smiled and hugged Daisy around the waist.

After four years of service at the Driehoek Home for Girls, Daisy was promoted to the rank of Major. Commenting on this promotion, one of her comrades wrote:

Patience and tact can well be said to be the outstanding characteristics of our recently promoted comrade, which have undoubtedly been of great value to the Major in her Salvation Army career. The Major accepted the appointment to become Matron at the Driehoek Home for Girls four years ago, and has proved to be an ideal Matron. The children look upon her as a mother, and many a child coming from a parentless home—or worse—has been comforted and helped by the Major's loving attention; while those girls whose every good feeling has been stifled because of evil surroundings, have blossomed out through her love and prayers.

Major Scott finds consolation in her own children, who all sought the Lord early—two of whom are in the Salvation Army. Percy is a Captain at the Benoni Corps, while Walter is a Bandsman at Germiston. All honour to the Major for her courageous and devoted service, and hearty congratulations on her promotion.

In 1929 South Africa found itself in the grip of a worldwide depression, following the collapse of the New York Stock Exchange in October. People lost their jobs, businesses went bankrupt, doctors and lawyers were seen digging trenches in streets in order to earn some money, and many people lost their homes and had to live in fields under flimsy shelters constructed from whatever building materials they could find.

The South African Railways employed as many extra workmen as they could and the Government employed workers to reclaim the foreshore at Cape Town.

The Salvation Army in South Africa found itself struggling to cope with the steady stream of needy people looking for help. They set up soup kitchens and fed as many people as possible throughout the country. In the Driehoek Home for Girls, Daisy engaged the older girls in preparing vegetables for the soup that was made each day to feed the steadily rising number of desperate people looking for food.

This worldwide Great Depression lasted for several years, causing much hardship and despair. Many women went out to work for the first time, taking whatever lowly paid job they could find, and the number of young girls admitted to the Home increased.

"We'll just do the best we can, and trust God to guide us in our work," Daisy remarked to Polly.

"Bad times don't last forever," Polly replied, "and one of these days the situation will improve."

"You always see the sunshine through the rain, don't you?" Daisy smiled, giving her sister a hug.

Polly was right, for in 1931 Britain came off the gold standard. Jan Smuts, Leader of the Opposition in the South African Parliament, persuaded the South African Government to follow suit. The results were heartening; mines that were considering closing decided to remain open as gold jumped to almost double the price. Ore that had been thought useless was now mined, providing much needed employment, and slowly the country returned to a normal way of life.

But the hard lessons learned during those dark days of the Great Depression remained with people for the rest of their lives. Forced to live frugally in order to survive, they learned to save for a 'rainy day.'

CHAPTER 23

SHE LEFT MORE SUNSHINE THAN SHE FOUND

Early in 1933 Daisy found herself being transferred once more, this time to Johannesburg, to take up the position of Matron of the Young Women's Hostel.

Polly, by this time elderly and declining in health, needed care and attention, and it was arranged for her to live at the Hostel with Daisy. Polly was soon well liked by the young women, who found that despite her ailments she was never too tired to listen to their problems and give them a word of cheer.

Gradually, as time went by, Polly became more frail and sickly and was eventually bedridden. Daisy spent long hours each day caring for her sister, until at the age of seventy-nine, after an illness lasting four years, Polly passed away on July 27th, 1936.

In a moving tribute to her sister, Daisy wrote:

Standing at the bedside of my dear sister, watching her passing so peacefully over to her eternal home, I thanked God that she had gone into the presence of her Lord, whom she had loved and served so faithfully.
My sister lived for others. She had no thought for herself. All her life she sought after the fallen, the despised, and those for whom no one cared.

*She did not shine on the platform, but in the dark
places, and in the haunts of sin and vice. She carried
a message of hope and love. She was never too busy nor
too weary to help anyone in need, and she believed in
the power of God to save the very worst.*

*A few years ago she wrote these words in a friend's
autograph book:*

*'Let it be said of me when underground
She left more sunshine than she found.'*

*Wherever she went she scattered sunshine, and there
will forever remain with us the sweet influence of her
life. She has fought the fight and won the race, and I
think that on the Eternal Morning the King will say
to her: 'Inasmuch as ye have done it unto one of the
least of these my brethren, ye have done it unto Me.'
"Auntie" Quarterman, as she was affectionately
termed far beyond the bounds of her own circle of
nephews and nieces, will long be remembered by all
who knew her.*

For the first time in her life, Daisy's older sister was no longer there. Looking back, she thought of the heady days in London, when she had marched through the streets with Polly, holding her hand tightly while the band marched ahead of them, playing their instruments. Polly had always been there, guiding and helping her, and she would miss her wise counsel.

But life had to continue, and Daisy was kept busy with her work. All her children, who by now were married and had families of their own, came to visit her as often as possible, 'Gran' being a great favourite with her grandchildren. She could always be counted on to produce a tin of tasty 'bull's eyes' that she kept for 'good' children, a distinction for which each child miraculously seemed to qualify.

The influence that Daisy had over others was evident in her own family, many of whom were actively engaged in Christian work. Her eldest son Jim had married Gwen Volkwyn and lived in Rhodesia with their three children, Daisy Jr. had married Francis Partridge and had two children, and Percy, an Officer in the Salvation Army, was married to fellow Officer Ivy Tripp. Wally, the youngest, was married to Dorothy Brown, and despite having a family of seven children, they still found time to work among young people.

On December 12th, 1938, after having been in charge of the Young Women's Hostel for over five years, Daisy retired from Active Service as an Officer. Almost sixty-one years old, she felt the need to visit her sister Nellie, now aged seventy-one, and her brother James' family in England.

A large farewell social was arranged which was attended by many of her life-long friends, boarders and staff from the Hostel.

Daisy looked slowly around the group of Officers seated before her, many of whom had shared her toil, her joys and her sorrow. They were her kind of people. She had spent a lifetime in service with them—and now it was time to say farewell.

Commissioner Cunningham, addressing the gathering, paid tribute to Daisy for her forty-two years of unbroken service in South Africa since arriving from England in 1896. He referred to her diligent work before and after her marriage to Staff-Captain Walter Scott, and how she had made a lasting impression on the lives of many people. He then presented her with a beautifully designed, framed Citation, which read as follows:

The William Booth Memorial Hostel.
To Major Mrs. Scott.

Dear Comrade,
On the occasion of your retirement from Active Service as an Officer, the Army desires to in this way place on record its grateful thanks for forty-two years of devoted and exemplary service rendered by you since coming to South Africa as an Officer in 1896.
Prior to your marriage you served faithfully and successfully as a Field Officer, and afterwards with your noble and brave husband (now in the Glory Land) you proved yourself a worthy helpmate and today your own, and the children of others for whom you have cared so tenderly, love you and call you blessed.
Your courage in bereavement and your untiring efforts to rise above sorrow and difficulty, pressing on with your work for God and the Army, have won you our highest esteem. All over South Africa comrades and friends regret that the time should have come for you to retire from active participation in the work you have done so well and loved so much.
Unitedly we pray that the evening of your busy life will prove restful and pleasant to you, and we hope that a gracious Heavenly Father will long stay the sun from going down, so that you may for many years be among us as a happy and blessed Mother in Israel.
Wishing you God's choicest and continuous blessings,
Yours on behalf of comrades of all ranks,

J. Cunningham,
COMMISSIONER
Johannesburg.
12.12.1938.

With her Salvation Army career finally over, Daisy was free to think of her own family ties. Nellie, now an aged and sickly spinster living in a house with another elderly woman in England, was Daisy's main concern. There was no-one close by to care for her should she become ill, so with this problem in mind Daisy decided to visit Nellie and make arrangements for her future.

As the Union Castle liner docked in Southampton, the old familiar thrill returned at the sight of her homeland, last visited so many years before with Walter. Travelling in the train to London, Daisy looked out of the window at the unchanged little villages as they passed by, with the steeples of the churches presiding over them. Those little villages, with their winding, narrow streets and rows of houses joined together, were as pretty as ever, she thought.

Nellie was overjoyed to see her sister after so long an absence, and although they had corresponded regularly over the years, they nevertheless had much to tell each other.

After a few days, Daisy broached the subject of Nellie moving into an Old Aged Home, where Daisy knew she would be well cared for.

"I'm concerned about you, Nellie," she said, "because I live so far away and you will have nobody to care for you if you become ill. I think you would be well cared for in the Salvation Army Retirement Home in Lewes, in the county of Sussex."

After some protests Nellie eventually agreed to Daisy's proposal and the task of sorting through her belongings had begun when Daisy came across a bundle of old letters that she had written to Nellie over the years, describing her experiences in South Africa.

"You don't need these old letters, Nellie. They're of no use to you now. Let's throw them away," said Daisy, and in her usual practical way she threw them into the waste paper basket.

No sooner had Daisy sorted out Nellie's affairs when a telegram arrived in August from her daughter Daisy, informing her that her husband Francis had passed away. Realizing that her daughter needed her to help care for her two young children, she decided to return immediately to South Africa.

Europe was in a state of political turmoil with the ominous rumblings of a second World War becoming more real by the day. On several occasions Daisy booked a passage on a ship bound for South Africa, only to have it cancelled at the last moment.

Hitler's forces invaded Poland on September lst, 1939 and Britain and France declared war. The Second World War began in earnest.

Daisy realized that if she didn't get a passage to South Africa immediately, she would be forced to remain in England. Eventually, after a sad farewell to Nellie, she was able to board the *Llanstephan Castle*, a rickety old ship almost due for the scrapyard, which left Southampton in September.

The journey across the ocean was a nightmare. The old ship creaked and groaned and had to zig-zag across the Atlantic, many miles off course, to avoid possible German submarines.

Ironically, it was not the submarines that caused concern amongst the passengers, but a natural phenomenon. One afternoon without warning a giant wave struck the ship, rocking it violently and tossing the panic-stricken passengers about. Chairs and tables slid across the floor and crashed against the wall.

The Captain on the bridge thought their last hour had come. But there was life in the old ship yet. Defying the elements, she managed to stabilize herself and continued on her journey, creaking and groaning all the more.

Chatting to fellow passengers after order had been restored and the ship's doctor had finished treating passengers for injuries, Daisy couldn't help but chuckle.

"As a girl I longed for adventure," she remarked, "and I'm still finding it—even at the age of sixty-one!"

The passengers were relieved when the ship eventually docked in Cape Town, where they enjoyed the welcome sight of Table Mountain bathed in sunlight, with a wisp of cloud drifting over its summit.

Memories came flooding back to Daisy. So many years ago she had stood on the deck of the *Tintagel Castle*, admiring that same scene and wondering what this new land had in store for her. Over forty years had passed since that day—busy, eventful years during which she had met and married Walter, with whom she had spent nine happy years.

But there was no time for reflection. She would soon be on a train bound for Johannesburg, where her daughter and her children would be waiting for her, and another page in the story of her life would begin.

Daisy lived with her daughter Daisy Jr. in Johannesburg for many years, helping to bring up her two children while she went to work at the University.

The Second World War raged across Europe and Britain, with South Africa, along with many other countries, supporting Britain by sending troops. Women once again played an important role in running essential services and sending parcels to the troops "up north."

Daisy's son Wally joined the South African Air Force, where he served as a photographer, and Percy served as an Officer in the Salvation Army. The war, which caused untold misery and destruction and cost millions of lives, eventually ended in 1945.

Daisy, in the meantime, saw as much as she could of her large family, and later lived with each of her other children, enjoying a peaceful retirement and comparative good health.

On 21st February 1968 Daisy celebrated her ninetieth birthday at the home of her grandson, Doug Scott, the son of Wally and Dolly. Over a hundred relatives and friends, who had travelled from as far afield as Cape Town and Salisbury, were present to wish her well.

Among the distinguished guests was Commissioner Carl Richards, Territorial Commander of the Salvation Army in South Africa, who paid tribute to Major Mrs. Scott for her outstanding service to others through her Salvation Army work, over a period of more than forty years.

Many of the children who were under her care at the Children's Home in Germiston were present as well. Some of them were now mothers themselves, but they still regarded Daisy as their "mother," and corresponded regularly with her.

Looking around the room she noted with satisfaction that all four of her children were there, as well as fifteen grandchildren and thirty great grandchildren.

When called upon to address those present, Daisy stood up and spoke for twenty minutes, recalling all the happy times she had had in the service of the Salvation Army over the years. When asked for her recipe for a happy life, she replied without hesitation: "Faith in God, a contented mind, living for others and a sense of humour."

Percy, Jim, Wally, Daisy Jr. and Daisy Scott,
on her ninetieth birthday, February 21st, 1968.

Daisy's last home was in Durban with her son Wally and daughter-in-law Dolly. Although her eyesight was poor she still corresponded regularly with her many friends all over the world—among them the girls who had been in her care at the Driehoek Home and the Young Women's Hostel. Her letters were always cheerful and inspiring, ending with an encouraging Bible quotation. Although her eyes were dim and she walked painfully slowly with the aid of a cane, her bright sense of humour still prevailed.

On April 27th, 1972, after a short illness, Daisy slipped away to join her beloved Walter. At the age of ninety-four years, she was the oldest Salvation Army Officer in South Africa.

Messages of condolence poured in from all parts of South Africa and overseas, many of them expressing gratitude for the help she had given.

Among those paying tribute at her funeral and memorial service were Colonel H.M. King, Lieut-Colonel J.T. Usher, Major E. Holmes and her own son, Lieut-Colonel Percy Scott (R).

In a letter of condolence to the Scott family, Colonel King, the Chief Secretary, paid a fitting tribute to this outstanding woman, who was loved not only by every member of the Scott family, but by countless friends all over the country and beyond its borders. He wrote:

> *We received news yesterday evening of the promotion to glory of your dear mother, and feel this is such a triumphant end that we must not mourn, but rejoice in a victorious life so fruitfully spent in the service of God.*
>
> *However, we know that you and your family will feel the passing of a mother who was so gracious and compassionate toward her family, and assure you all of our sincere prayers that God will sustain you in your bereavement, and also keep you faithful, as your mother was kept right to the very end.*
>
> *Your mother was one of the Army pioneers in this country, and this impact will never be forgotten. She becomes one of the heroines in the annals of Army history, and her example is one we should all endeavour to follow.*

Daisy Scott's legacy continues to this day, with many members of the Scott family actively engaged in Christian service in various parts of the world. Much loved "Gran Gran," as she was known to her family, is fondly remembered for her kindness and bright, cheerful spirit, as well as those dimples in her cheeks—those same dimples that had captured the heart of Walter so many years before.

The girl in a blue bonnet, marching confidently forward with a tambourine in her hand, will long be remembered for the way she inspired so many people to live better lives.

Sources of reference

The Salvation Army literature in Canada and South Africa.

History of South Africa by Prof. W.J. de Kock, Department of Information, Pretoria 1970.

Petticoat in Mafeking by John Midgley, Kommetjie, Cape Province, South Africa 1974.

The Boer War Diary of Sol T. Plaatje, Mac Millan South Africa, 1973.